烹饪英语
English for Cuisine

主　编　赵　丽
副主编　潘素玲　田雅琳
编　者　杨力红　鲜于静　王蕴喆

北京大学出版社
PEKING UNIVERSITY PRESS

图书在版编目(CIP)数据

烹饪英语 / 赵丽主编. —北京：北京大学出版社，2010.3
（全国职业技能英语系列教材）
ISBN 978-7-301-13834-2

Ⅰ. 烹…　Ⅱ. 赵…　Ⅲ. 烹饪-英语-高等学校：技术学校-教材　Ⅳ. H31

中国版本图书馆CIP数据核字（2008）第067928号

书　　　　名：	烹饪英语
著作责任者：	赵　丽　主编
责 任 编 辑：	刘　爽
标 准 书 号：	ISBN 978-7-301-13834-2/H·1997
出 版 发 行：	北京大学出版社
地　　　　址：	北京市海淀区成府路205号　100871
网　　　　址：	http://www.pup.cn
电　　　　话：	邮购部 62752015　发行部 62750672　编辑部 62767315　出版部 62754962
电 子 邮 箱：	zbing@pup.pku.edu.cn
印 　刷　 者：	三河市北燕印装有限公司
经 　销　 者：	新华书店
	787毫米×1092毫米　16开本　15.75印张　374千字
	2010年3月第1版　2022年4月第9次印刷
定　　　　价：	45.00元（配有光盘）

未经许可，不得以任何方式复制或抄袭本书之部分或全部内容。
版权所有，侵权必究　举报电话：010-62752024
电子邮箱：fd@pup.pku.edu.cn

总 序

我国高职高专教育的春天到来了。随着国家对高职高专教育重视程度的加深,职业技能教材体系的建设已成为当务之急。高职高专过去沿用和压缩大学本科教材的时代一去不复返了。

语言学家 Harmer 指出:"如果我们希望学生学到的语言是在真实生活中能够使用的语言,那么在教材编写中接受技能和产出技能的培养也应该像在生活中那样有机地结合在一起。"

教改的关键在教师,教师的关键在教材,教材的关键在理念。我们依据《高职高专教育英语课程教学基本要求》的精神和编者做了大量调查,秉承"实用为主,够用为度,学以致用,触类旁通"的原则,历经两年艰辛,为高职高专学生编写了这套专业技能课和实训课的英语教材。

本套教材的内容贴近工作岗位,突出岗位情景英语,是一套职场英语教材,具有很强的实用性、仿真性、职业性,其特色体现在以下几个方面:

1. 开放性

   本套教材在坚持编写理念、原则及体例的前提下,不断增加新的行业或岗位技能英语分册作为教材的延续。

2. 国际性

   本套教材以国内自编为主,以国外引进为辅,取长补短,浑然一体。目前已从德国引进了某些行业的技能英语教材,还将从德国或他国引进优秀教材经过本土化后奉献给广大师生。

3. 职业性

   本套教材是由高校教师与行业专家针对具体工作岗位、情景过程共同设计编写,同时注重与行业资格证书相结合。

4. 任务性

   基于完成某岗位工作任务而需要的英语知识和技能是本套教材的由来与初衷。因此,各分册均以任务型练习为主。

5. 实用性

　　本教材注重基础词汇的复习和专业词汇的补充。适合于在校最后一学期的英语教学，着重培养和训练学生初步具有与其日后职业生涯所必需的英语交际能力。

　本教材在编写过程中，参考和引用了国内外作者的相关资料，得到了北京大学出版社外语编辑部的倾力奉献，在此，一并向他们表示敬意和感谢。由于本套教材是一种创新和尝试，书中瑕疵必定不少，敬请指正。

丁国声

教育部高职高专英语类专业教学指导委员会委员

河北省高校外语教学研究会副会长

河北外国语职业学院院长

2008 年 6 月

前 言

目前,我国高等职业教育发展迅速,已进入了优质教育和培养实用型人才教育模式的新阶段。教育部为高等职业教育提出了"实用为主,够用为度"的原则,反映了社会对实用型人才的需求,明确了高等职业教育的办学宗旨。

高等职业教育从本质上讲就是就业教育。随着行业对从业人员英语应用能力要求的不断提高,高等职业专业英语教育应紧密结合行业的实际,强调英语实际应用的能力,使学习者能将所学到的知识应用到行业中去,培养社会所需求的有用人才。

为了适应社会的需要,我们编写了《烹饪英语》一书,本教材符合高等职业教育的宗旨,以先进的教学理念为指导,以能力培养为本位,以就业为导向,遵循专业英语的教学规律,紧密结合行业的实际,把语言教学和职业教育融为一体,突显了高等职业教育的特点,体现了学以致用的教学原则。

《烹饪英语》一书,按照高等职业教育英语教学的性质和目标要求,以食品制作、菜肴制作岗位为背景,围绕烹饪工作任务设计教学内容,具有鲜明的针对性。本教材内容全面、新颖独特、实用性强,情景设置与烹饪工作人员的实际工作密切相关,涵盖了实际工作的各个环节,突出了实际操作的特点。本教材遵循功能语言学的教学原理,采用任务型教学模式,注重语言技能与职业知识技能的整合,加大了语言的输出量,体现了"在做中学"的教学理念。本教材适用于餐饮、烹饪管理专业学生及有意于从事餐饮行业工作的有识之士。

《烹饪英语》共分 10 个单元,每个单元由 Part A 和 Part B 两部分构成,每个部分围绕一个主题展开,以贴近烹饪操作流程的内容为主线,创设真实的交流情景,以活泼有趣、形式多样、激发创造力的教学活动为学习者提供了最大限度的交流实践机会,使学习者有充分的时间运用所学的专业英语进行交际。每部分由 *Start You Off; Focus on Language; Summarize Key Expressions; Give It a Try* 和 *Do Extension Activities* 五项内容组成。教学重点清晰明确,易于教学,内容组织科学合理,循序渐进,每项内容后均配有相关的练习,并配有详实的答案供学习和教学参考。本教材的编写和设计强调实践性,培养学生自主学习的能力。学生的任务是主动地、创造性地参与学习过程,引导学生发挥主体作用,通过各种课堂活动,运用自己掌握的知识和交际能力,主动地与他人交流所学习的语言,从而达到学以致用的目的。

《烹饪英语》一书由北京联合大学旅游学院赵丽教授担任主编,潘素玲、田雅琳为副主编。参加编写的人员还有:杨力红、鲜于静、王蕴喆。赵丽负责本教材内容、结构编排设计、全书统稿及第2单元的编写工作。第1单元由王蕴喆编写;第3、7、8单元由潘素玲编写;第4、5单元由杨力红编写;第6单元由鲜于静编写;第9、10单元由田雅琳编写。

由于时间仓促,编者水平有限,书中不当之处在所难免,恳请专家和读者不吝赐教。

编者

2009年3月

Contents

Unit 1	**Kitchen Introduction**	1
	Part A Titles and Job Description	1
	Part B Kitchen Rules	12

Unit 2	**Kitchen Facilities**	21
	Part A Floor Plan and Kitchen Equipment	21
	Part B Tools and Utensils for Food Production	31

Unit 3	**Condiments**	47
	Part A Sauce, Paste & Powdered Condiments	47
	Part B Spices	54

Unit 4	**Food Material I**	61
	Part A BOM	61
	Part B Vegetable Process	69

Unit 5	**Food Material II**	77
	Part A BOM	77
	Part B Fruit Process	84

Unit 6	**Food Material III**	90
	Part A Beef and Lamb	90
	Part B Poultry and Seafood	102

Unit 7	**Making a Meal**	111
	Part A Making an Appetizer	111
	Part B Making Soup	119

Unit 8	**Making a Dish**	130
	Part A Making Western Food	130
	Part B Making Western & Chinese Food	139

Unit 9	**Dessert**	147
	Part A Making a Dessert I	147
	Part B Making a Dessert II	155

Unit 10	**Food Safety**	164
	Part A Food Contamination	164
	Part B Food Spoilage and Preservation	171

Vocabulary 179
Key to Exercises 186
Tapescript 218
Reference 239

Unit 1

Kitchen Introduction

Part A Titles and Job Description

Teaching hours: 2 hours

LEARNING GOALS

To be able to
* ask about one's job
* describe one's job
* know job titles in the kitchen
* know job duties in the kitchen

VOCABULARY ASSISTANCE

cook	n.	厨师	title	n.	头衔, 官衔, 职别
gardener	n.	园丁	kitchen	n.	厨房
mechanic	n.	技工, 机修工	executive	adj. & n.	执行的; 执行者
reporter	n.	记者, 通讯员	chef	n.	厨师长
doctor	n.	医生; 博士	assistant	adj. & n.	助理的; 助理
waiter	n.	男服务员	sous-chef	n.	[法]副厨师长
policeman	n.	警察	larder	n.	食品室, 餐具室
athlete	n.	运动员, 运动选手	pastry	n.	面点
barber	n.	理发员, 理发师	vegetable	n.	植物, 蔬菜
benefit / perk	n.	利益, 额外津贴	butcher	n. & v.	屠夫; 屠宰
promotion	n.	提拔, 晋升	sauce	n.	调味汁, 调味料
flexi-time	n.	弹性上班制	soup	n.	汤
bonus	n.	奖金, 红利	pension	n.	养老金, 退休金
apprentice	n.	徒弟, 学徒工	pantryman	n.	配膳员, 食品管理者
potman	n.	擦洗锅的人	porter	n.	搬运工人
steward	n.	厨房清扫工人	relief	n.	换班者, 接班者
boring	adj.	令人厌烦的	repetitive	adj.	重复的, 反复性的

rewarding	adj.	报答的,有益的,值得的
challenging	adj.	引起挑战性兴趣的,挑逗的
satisfying	adj.	令人满足的,令人满意的
stressful	adj.	产生压力的,使紧迫的
grill	n. & v.	铁箅子;烤炙室;烤炙
roast	n. & v.	烤肉;烤,煨,烘,焙,炒
staff	n.	工作人员(全体),职员(全体)
aboyeur	n.	[法]跑堂喊菜的人
commis	n.	实习侍者,助理厨师
executive chef		行政总厨师长
assistant chef		行政总厨师长助理
larder chef		负责烹饪各种肉类的厨师长
grill cook		负责在烤架上烤炙肉类的厨师
career ladder		职务级别提升,(职务)提级

Start You Off

Activity 1

Look at the pictures below and do the question and answer practice in pairs.

A: **What do you do? / What do you do for a living?**

B: **I'm a/an _____.**

1. cook

2. gardener

3. mechanic

4. waiter

5. reporter

6. doctor

7. policeman

8. athlete

9. barber

Unit 1

Activity 2

Read the sentences and then put the phrases underlined into the correct list below.

1. I work very long hours.
2. I get a company car.
3. They've got a good pension scheme.
4. I'm hoping to get promoted next year.
5. You can work your way up quite quickly.
6. I get a regular pay rise.
7. I can go part-time after I've had my baby.
8. I'm taking a few days off next week. The kids are off school.
9. I'm ambitious. I want to move up the career ladder.
10. They give us a bonus at Christmas.
11. It isn't very well-paid.
12. I get six week's paid holiday.
13. I'm on a pretty good salary.
14. I can do overtime if I like.
15. They run a system of flexi-time.
16. I get private health insurance.

Money
_____
_____
_____
_____

Hours
_____
_____
_____
_____

Benefits / Perks
_____
_____
_____

Promotion
_____
_____
_____

Holiday
_____
_____

Focus on Language

Conversation

Listen to the conversation and read after it. Then try to find the answers to the questions.

Talking about Family Members' Job

Questions:
1. What does Aribella's second eldest sister do?
2. What does Aribella's father do for a living? And what does he think of his job?
3. What does Aribella's mother do? And what does she work for?

1. Asking about the occupation

- ◆ What do you do?
- ◇ I am a/an...
- ◆ What do you do for a living?
- ◇ I work for.../ I work in...

Task 1

Look at the pictures below and practise in pairs using the sentence structures in 'Asking about the occupation.'

A: What do you do in the kitchen?
B: I'm a/an_____ .

Executive Chef or Head Chef   Assistant Chef or Second Chef

Unit 1

Sous-Chefs

Larder Chef

Pastry Chef

Vegetable Chef

Section Heads

Sauce Cook

Soup Cook

Vegetable Cook

Grill Cook

Roast Cook

Fish Cook

Breakfast Cook

Night Cook

Relief Cook

Other Positions

Aboyeur or Caller

Commis (Apprentice) Cook

Potman

      Steward   Butcher   pantryman

Look at the pictures below and practise in pairs using the sentence structures in 'Asking about the occupation.

A: What do you do for a living?
B: I work for.../ I work in...

   Grand Hotel (Beijing)   Beijing Landmark Hotel

The following form shows people who work in the kitchen of Beijing Hotel. Look at the form below, try to find out what they do and write down the names of their duties.

TERM	DEFINITION
	The person who can relieve everyone.
	The person who works between cook and guest, and carries orders to the cook.
	The person who makes the breakfast.
	The person who cuts the meat and slaughters the animals.
	The person who washes pans and pots.
	The person who puts the meat into the oven.
	The person who is responsible for the pantry.

Unit 1

2. Expressing your attitudes toward your job

◆ How long do you work every day?
◇ Around 10 hours.
◆ How do you find / What do you think of your job?
◇ I think it is very… / I believe it is so… / I suppose it is too… / I find it…

Task 1

The sentences below describe what you like or dislike about your job. Match the beginnings with endings.

1. I hate having to attend
2. I love meeting
3. I wish I didn't have to do
4. I run my own business. I really enjoy being
5. I hate having to deal with
6. I get on really well with

a. so much boring paperwork.
b. my own boss.
c. new people.
d. difficult customers.
e. so many meetings.
f. all of my colleagues except one.

Task 2

Two friends haven't seen each other for a long time, now they are meeting in a café and talking about their jobs. Make a conversation in pairs.

A: How do you find your job? / What do think of your job?
B: My job is so.... / It's very... / I find it very...
A: Why is it so...? / Why is it very...? / Why do you find it... ?
B: Because...

 boring / Because it's the same thing day after day.

 repetitive / Because I just sit there all day filling in forms.

 satisfying / Because it's very satisfying to know that you've helped somebody through their exams.

rewarding / Because knowing that I might have saved somebody's life is very rewarding.

challenging / Because it requires a lot of concentration and determination.

stressful / Because it's making me ill.

3. Talking about your job duties

◆ What do you do as a /an…?
◇ I am responsible for…
◆ And what about you? / How about you?
◇ I'm in charge of…

Work in pairs and make a short conversation with the information in the box. Follow the model given below.

A: What do you do as a/an …?
B: I am responsible for/in charge of …
A: How long do you work everyday?
B: Around / about…
A: How do you find / What do you think of your job?
B: I hate / love…

Job Title	Central Kitchen Aide
Duty	Assists in preparing the quantity of pre-plated meals necessary for service
Working Hours	9 hours
Attitude toward Work	Loving

Job Title	Kitchen Porter
Duty	Performs simple manual work in maintaining a clean and orderly kitchen
Working Hours	6 hours
Attitude toward Work	Stressful

Unit 1

Job Title	General Kitchen Assistant
Duty	Performs all aspects of kitchen duties as directed by the cook
Working Hours	7 hours
Attitude toward Work	Satisfying

Summarize Key Expressions

1. **Talking about your occupation**
   a. What do you do?
      I am a/an...
   b. What do you do for living?
      I work for.../I work in...

2. **Talking about your job**
   a. How do you find in your job?
   b. What do you think of your job?
   c. How about your job?

3. **Expressing your attitudes toward your job**
   a. I think it is very attractive/satisfying/ boring...
   b. I believe it is so attractive/satisfying/ boring...
   c. I find it very attractive/satisfying/ boring...

4. **Describing your job duties**
   a. What do you do as a/an...?
   b. What are you in charge of...?
   c. What are you responsible for...?

Give It a Try

Task 1

Ask about what your partner does and, if appropriate, where he/she works.

A: What do you do?
B: _____
A: Oh, really? What company do you work for/in?
B: _____, and you?
A: Oh, I am a/an _____

Task 2

Now change the roles and do Task 1 again.

Task 3

You are Natalia Wolinsky who is a reporter doing a survey in a restaurant where you work. Answer the reporter's questions.

Reporter: Tell me a bit about your job. What do you do in the restaurant?
Natalia: _____
Reporter: I see, and what do you do as a / an _____?
Natalia: _____
Reporter: Do you know what a potman does?
Natalia: Yes, _____?
Reporter: What do you think of your job?
Natalia: _____
Reporter: How do you find a potman's job?
Natalia: _____

Do Extension Activities

Activity 1

A Community Committee is conducting questionnaires on the kitchen jobs. Fill in the form below and explain to the community about the information.

Community Committee
1. Sex: male☐ female☐
2. Marital status: single☐ married☐
3. Occupation: _____
4. Annual income: _____
5. Responsibilities: _____
6. Working hours: _____
7. Attitudes towards the job: _____

Unit 1

Activity 2

Work in groups of three and introduce your friends to one another. Follow the model given below.

A: Sophie { is a/an _____.
           { works for _____.

B: Oh,   { really?
           { are you?

C: Yes,   { I work for _____. And what do you do, Russell?
           { I am a / an _____.

B: Oh,   { I am a / an _____.
           { I work in _____.

Learning Tips

Kitchen Sanitation and Safety I

★ Clean and sanitize all food contact surfaces prior to starting work and after work is finished.

★ Disposable gloves are to be worn when handling ready-to-eat food.

★ No detergents or chemicals allowed in food production area. Cleaning supplies will be stored and locked in the maintenance room.

★ All laundry including towels, labcoats, aprons, etc., must be placed in laundry baskets in the restrooms when necessary at the completion of production. Do not use any laundry that has already been placed in the laundry baskets.

Part B Kitchen Rules

Teaching hours: 2 hours

LEARNING GOALS

To be able to
* ask and explain the working procedure
* ask work requirements in the kitchen
* ask and tell what should be done

VOCABULARY ASSISTANCE

rule	n.	规则,惯例,章程	deliver	v.	递送,释放
handkerchief	n.	手帕,纸巾	facility	n.	设施,设备
include	v.	包括,包含	beard	n.	胡须
remove	v.	移开,拿开	procedure	n.	程序,手续
boil	n. & v.	沸点;沸腾;煮沸	stove	n.	炉
lather	n. & v.	肥皂泡;涂以肥皂泡	scrub	v.	洗擦,擦净
rinse	v.	(用清水)刷,冲洗掉	cough	v.	咳嗽
sneeze	v.	打喷嚏	garbage	n.	垃圾,废物
sweep	v.	扫,打扫,清扫	mop	v.	用拖把拖洗,擦
equipment	n.	装备,设备,器材	hairnet	n.	发网
supply	n.	补给,供给,供应品	sink	n.	水槽,水池
wipe	v.	擦,擦去	ventilation	n.	通风,流通空气
utensil	n.	器具	surrender	v.	交出;放弃,听任
license	n.	执照,许可证,特许	cooker	n.	炊具,蒸(煮)机
valid	adj.	[律]有效的,正当的	pot	n.	罐,壶
peeling	n.	剥皮;剥下的皮	burner	n.	火炉;烧火的人
wrapper	n.	包装材料,包装纸	waste bin		废物箱,垃圾箱
container	n.	容器(箱、盆、罐、壶、桶、坛子)			

Unit 1

Start You Off

Activity

Ask your partner how to cook some rice, use the cues given below and put them in the right order.

— How to... ?
— First...
— Then you...
— And after that you...

▶ Put the rice in a pot
▶ Bring it to the boil again and cook it slowly for about 20 minutes
▶ Wash the rice in cold water
▶ Cover it with water

Focus on Language

Listening

Personal Health Cleanliness and Safety in the Kitchen

Listen to the recording and fill in the blanks with the missing words you will hear.

1. Hands must be _____ before starting work, after handling food, after _____, after _____ the toilet and after using a _____ or tissue. The hand _____ in the production area must be used for hand washing. The sink in the restroom must be used after using the restroom _____. Hands must be washed with _____ soapy water for a minimum of 20 _____ and dried with a _____ towel.

2. All cuts _____ be bandaged _____ waterproof protectors, and watertight disposable gloves _____ be worn.

3. _____ staff with _____ lesions, infected wounds, _____ throats or any

13

communicable diseases shall _____ be permitted to _____ in the kitchen.

4. _____ eating _____ drinking permitted in the kitchen area. No _____ of tobacco products allowed in the kitchen.

5. Kitchen staff shall be _____ and well groomed. Clothing should be _____ of a washable fabric. No open-toed _____ are to be _____ in the kitchen.

6. All the kitchen staff is to _____ hair restraints provided by the kitchen. This _____ the use of both _____ and _____ nets as necessary.

7. Personal belongings _____ be kept out of food preparation and storage areas. All personal belongings _____ to be stored in the designated area or off premises.

8. _____ all insecure jewelry that might fall _____ food or equipment. Remove hand jewelry when manipulating food by hand.

##

1. Asking about the procedure

◆ How to…?
◇ First…
◆ Then…
◇ After that you…

Task 1

Look at the pictures below, use the word and picture cues and explain to your partner how to wash hands.

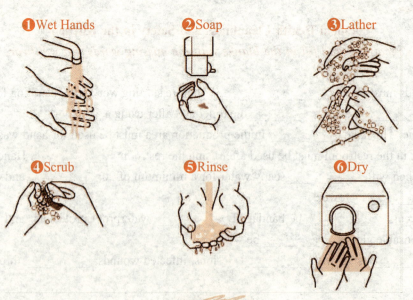

❶ Wet Hands ❷ Soap ❸ Lather
❹ Scrub ❺ Rinse ❻ Dry

Unit 1

How to wash your hands:

First, _____ your hands with clean running water and use soap. Use warm water if it is available.

Second, _____ your hands.

Third, _____ hands together to make a lather.

Then, _____ all surfaces.

Next, _____ hands well under running water.

Finally, _____ your hands using a paper towel or air dryer.

Task 2

Read the expressions below and practise in pairs asking your partner about when you should wash hands.

A: When should I wash my hands?
B: Before/ after...

- preparing food
- going to the bathroom
- blowing your nose, coughing or sneezing
- handling garbage
- treating a cut or wound

2. Ask work requirements in the kitchen

◆ Do I need to ...?
◆ Do I have to ...?
◆ Is it necessary to...?
◇ Yes, you have to...
◇ Yes, you need to ...
◇ No, you don't have to...
◇ No, you don't need to...
◇ No, it isn't necessary.

Task 1

You are talking to a restaurant manager. Ask the manager whether you have to do these things, using the cues below.

▶ *sweep and mop the floor*
▶ *clean equipments regularly*
▶ *make food preparation*

- ▶ wear hairnets
- ▶ take kitchen supplies home
- ▶ wash the dishes
- ▶ wash hands before cooking

Task 2

Now change the roles and do Task 1 again.

3. Say what should be done

◆ What should / must be done or noticed?
◇ ... must/ should be ...
◇ ... can't be ...

Task 1

There is a new Commis (Apprentice) Cook coming in the kitchen. He doesn't know the rules in the kitchen, now the General Kitchen Assistant is telling him what should / must be done or noticed. Work in pairs like this:

C = Commis (Apprentice) Cook   G = General Kitchen Assistant
C: What should / must be done or noticed?
G: Floors must be swept and mopped.

- ▶ *Sinks must be cleaned after use.*
- ▶ *Dish sink and surrounding areas should be cleaned and wiped dry after use.*
- ▶ *Clean clothing and close-toed shoes must be worn while working in the kitchen.*
- ▶ *Kitchen doors cannot be propped open but the doors on the North and South sides can be lifted for ventilation purposes.*

Task 2

A new employee (Mike) is asking his employer (George) about rules and regulations in the kitchen. Follow the example below to make sentences in pairs.

Mike: Am I allowed to smoke in the kitchen?
George: No, you're not allowed/ permitted.
Mike: Can I stack boxes or food supplies on the floors?

George: No, you cannot.

▶ *Kitchen supplies cannot be taken home.*
▶ *Kitchen doors cannot be propped open but the doors on the North and South sides can be lifted for ventilation purposes.*
▶ *Kitchen utensils cannot be borrowed.*
▶ *Proper food preparation cannot be postponed.*
▶ *You are not allowed to wear shorts in the restaurant.*

Summarize Key Expressions

1. **Talking about the procedure**
   a. First...
   b. Then...
   c. After that you...

2. **Ask work requirements in the kitchen**
   a. Do I need to...?
   b. Do I have to...?
   c. Is it necessary to...?

3. **Ask and tell what should be done**
   a. What should / must be done or noticed?
   b. ...must/ should be...
   c. ...can't be...

Give It a Try

Task 1

You are talking to one of the staff in the university library. Ask about what students can and cannot do, using the cues below.

▶ Smoke in the reading room
▶ Borrow books on reserve
▶ Take magazines home
▶ Borrow records
▶ Eat in the library
▶ Make a photocopy of newspaper articles

- Damage or destroy any library property
- Comply with all notices or signs in a library or on the library's website

LIBRARY RULES

- No food or drink.
- No smoking in the reading rooms.
- Magazines and reserved books may not be borrowed.
- Students may borrow up to four books at a time.
- Records and cassettes may not be borrowed.
- Articles and parts of books may not be copied for personal use.
- No damage or destroy of any Library property.
- All notices or signs in a library or on the library's website must be complied with.

Task 2

Read these rules about driving in the State of Mississippi.

a. It is not obligatory to wear seat belts in the State of Mississippi.
b. You must surrender all other drivers' licenses before being issued a Mississippi State driving license.
c. Foreign driving licenses can be used for up to one year.
d. A valid driving license from Canada can be used in Mississippi.
e. You must have a valid driving license with you at all times when you drive in Mississippi.

Student A is going to ask a question with the cues given below and Student B is going to answer the question using the model.

A: Is it all right to _____ ? / Can I _____ ?
B: No, you can't. You _____ . / Yes, you can.

- Drive without a seat belt
- Keep my old driving license
- Drive with a Canada license
- Use a foreign license in Mississippi
- Leave my license at home when I drive

Unit 1

Do Extension Activities

Activity 1

Look at the picture below. Joan's parents are visiting her this afternoon and her kitchen is in a terrible mess. Fill in the gaps in the sentences with the verbs given below.

| clear | throw out | empty | clean | put |

1. She should _____ the cooker.
2. She'll have to _____ the table.
3. She ought to _____ the waste bin.
4. She should _____ his coat away.
5. She should _____ all the empty bottles.

Activity 2

Do the questions and practise asking and answering by using the cues given below.

—"Is it all right to...?"
—"Yes, sure. / No, you shouldn't."

▶ throw away any wrappers, containers, peelings that you no longer want
▶ leave dirty dishes over night
▶ leave dirty pots on the stove after you are done using them
▶ use washcloths or paper towels to wash dishes
▶ cook on the stove if the burner is dirty

Learning Tips

Kitchen Sanitation and Safety II

★ Clean and sanitize all equipment according to posted instructions at the completion of production.

★ Cooler and freezer temperatures will be recorded daily by the manager. If dishwasher is used, wash water and rinse water temperatures must be recorded.

★ Only unopened packages and containers of food are to be brought into the kitchen.

★ All equipment brought into the kitchen must be washed and sanitized prior to use.

★ All raw meats shall be placed in covered containers and stored on the bottom shelf in the cooler or freezer.

Unit 2

Kitchen Facilities

Part A Floor Plan and Kitchen Equipment

Teaching hours: 2 hours

LEARNING GOALS

To be able to
* get familiar with the areas in the kitchen
* tell the names of the areas in the kitchen
* know the functions of the areas in the kitchen
* tell the names of the kitchen equipment

VOCABULARY ASSISTANCE

toaster	n.	烤面包机	drain	n.	排水管
refrigerator	n.	冰箱	dishwasher	n.	洗碗机
cupboard	n.	橱柜	oven	n.	烤箱
counter	n.	操作台	microwave	n.	微波炉
flammable	adj.	易燃的	broiler	n.	烤炉
indispensable	adj.	不可缺少的	disposal	n.	处理,处置
mincer/grinder	n.	绞肉机	sanitation	n.	卫生设备
mixer	n.	搅拌器	blender	n.	绞碎机
drainage	n.	排水系统;污水	bake	v.	烘制,烤制
hose	v.	用水管冲洗	fry top/grill		烤架
accessible	adj.	可进入的	deep frier/fryer		油炸锅,深炸(油)锅
grease	n.	油脂	frying basket		油炸篮(筐),沥油网篮
tub	n.	水龙头	egg boiler		煮蛋器
stopper	n.	塞子	food processor		加工器

Start You Off

Activity 1

Read the following numbered English words and try to find out their Chinese versions.

1. Freezer	2. Cold Kitchen	3. Butchery	4. Pastry	5. Beverage Cooler
6. Kitchen Store	7. Chef's Office			9. Pick-up Area
		8. Hot Kitchen		
	10. Pot-washer	11. Vegetable Preparation	12. Fish Section	13. Scullery

1. _____
2. _____
3. _____
4. _____
5. _____
6. _____
7. _____
8. _____
9. _____
10. _____
11. _____
12. _____
13. _____

Activity 2

Read the following English words in column A and try to match them with the Chinese versions in column B.

A	B
1. executive chef	a. 喊菜的服务员
2. grill cook	b. 厨房唱单员
3. fish cook	c. 屠夫

4. pastry chef 　　　　　d. 服务员
5. vegetable chef 　　　e. 负责擦洗大深锅的人
6. butcher 　　　　　　 f. 厨房清扫工人
7. aboyeur 　　　　　　g. 负责烹饪鱼的厨师
8. commis 　　　　　　 h. 负责在烤架上烤炙肉类的厨师
9. kitchen clerk 　　　　i. 厨房搬运工
10. pot-man 　　　　　　j. 学徒工
11. kitchen porter 　　　k. 行政总厨师长
12. steward 　　　　　　l. 面点厨师
13. waiter 　　　　　　　m. 负责烹饪蔬菜的厨师

Focus on Language

Listening

Questions:

1. How many areas are there in the kitchen?
2. What are the names of the areas in the kitchen?
3. What are the functions of different areas?

Listen to the passage and try to find the answers to the questions. Then put them in the table below.

Areas in the Kitchen	Function of the Areas
_____ Area	
_____ Area	
_____ Area	

➡ **Language Tips**

1. Floor plan

Practice 1

Work in pairs. Look at the floor plan given below and try to find the answers to the following questions.

Freezer	Cold Kitchen	Butchery	Pastry	Beverage Cooler	
Kitchen Store/ Pantry Area	Chef's Office				Pick-up Area
		Hot Kitchen			
	Pot-washer	Vegetable Preparation	Fish Section	Scullery	

1. Where is the executive chef?
   He is in the _____.
2. Where is the grill cook?
   He is in the _____.
3. Where is the fish cook?
   He is in the _____.
4. Where is the pastry chef?
   He is in the _____.
5. Where is the vegetable chef?
   He is in the _____.
6. Where is the butcher?
   He is in the _____.
7. Where is the aboyeur?
   He is in the _____.
8. Where is the commis?
   He is in the _____.
9. Where is the kitchen clerk?
   He is in the _____.
10. Where is the pot-man?
    He is in the _____.
11. Where is the kitchen porter?
    He is in the _____.
12. Where is the steward?
    He is in the _____.
13. Where is the waiter?
    He is in the _____.

2. The equipment in the kitchen

Practice 1

Look at the pictures and give their names in English.

1._____

2._____

3._____

4._____

5._____

6._____

Unit 2

Practice 2

Look at the following pictures and find out their names in English.

3. The facilities in the cooking area

Practice 1

Look at the pictures below and write down the names of the facilities in English.

1. _____
2. _____
3. _____

4. _____
5. _____
6. _____

7. _____
8. _____
9. _____

Picture 1: _____
Picture 2: _____
Picture 3: _____
Picture 4: _____
Picture 5: _____
Picture 6: _____
Picture 7: _____
Picture 8: _____
Picture 9: _____

Summarize Key Expressions

1. Floor plan
   a. chef's office
   b. hot kitchen/cold kitchen
   c. fish section
   d. pastry
   e. vegetable preparation
   f. butchery
   g. pick-up area
   h. pantry area
   i. chef's office
   j. pot-washer
   k. kitchen store
   l. scullery
   m. beverage cooler

2. The equipment in the kitchen
   a. oven
   b. refrigerator
   c. cupboard
   d. counter
   e. ranger
   f. electric steamer
   g. sink
   h. tub
   i. drain
   j. stopper
   k. garbage disposal
   l. dishwasher

Unit 2

3. The facilities in the cooking area
   a. stove
   b. deep frier/fryer
   c. fry top/grill
   d. microwave
   e. mincer/grinder
   f. electric mixer
   g. blender
   h. broiler
   i. burner

Give It a Try

Task 1

Do the task in pairs. Look at the following pictures and figure out their names in English. Then try to tell what they are used for.

1. _____   Description:
                              _____
                              _____
                              _____
                              _____
                              _____
                              _____

2. _____   Description:
                              _____
                              _____
                              _____
                              _____
                              _____
                              _____

3. _____   Description:
                              _____
                              _____
                              _____
                              _____
                              _____
                              _____

4. _____   Description:
   _____
                            _____
                            _____
                            _____
                            _____

Task 2

Listen to the recording and complete the following passage with the missing words.

Where should we put the refrigerators in the kitchen? Refrigerators _____ _____(1) either _____(2), or _____(3) to prevent power failure _____(4). The _____(5) in the kitchen should be _____(6) because kitchen is _____(7). Also materials should not be flammable _____(8) is indispensable in the kitchen.

Task 3

Read the following passage and make a discussion in groups. Then try to figure out the answers to the following questions.

1. What should be taken into consideration in kitchen design?
2. Why are sanitation and safety important?

In kitchen design, the emphasis should be placed on the ventilation, floor and drainage. The amount of air inside should be greater than the amount outside so that fresh air can be pressed into the kitchen. And, the ventilation system should be capable of removing hot air and cooking odors and pumping in fresh and cool air. The materials used for the floor should be easily hosed and of slipping proof. Most restaurant kitchens have washable floors and walls of concrete, tile or plastic to be hosed. To prevent slipping on vegetable peelings or similar wastes, many kitchens are equipped with duck boards that are laid down in the work areas and removed when the kitchen is washed. Drains are spaced to carry off the water efficiently. The dish and pot washing area should be located so that it is accessible from both the dining room and the kitchen. Busboys bring soiled dishes to the dishwashers who separate dishes from silver from glassware. They scrape any remaining food from the dishes so it is necessary to have equipment for waste disposal in the area. Sinks should be properly equipped for melting frozen food and soaking pots that have to be washed by hand. One of the biggest dangers in a kitchen comes from grease which is highly flammable. All equipment, like ovens or ranges on which the actual cooking is done, where a build-up of grease can occur must be carefully cleaned every day.

Do Extension Activities

Activity 1

Read the following English words in column A and try to match them with the Chinese versions in column B.

A	B
1. Gardemanger	a. 蒸笼工
2. Pastry Chef	b. 煎炸工
3. Rotisseur(grill)	c. 厨房唱单员
4. Saucier	d. 厨房帮工
5. Barbecue Cook	e. 厨房杂工
6. Chief Butcher	f. 厨房主管
7. Second Butcher	g. 面包师傅
8. Baker	h. 冷盘总厨师
9. Kitchen Supervisor	i. 糕饼师
10. Kitchen Hand	j. 烧烤厨师
11. Kitchen Helper	k. 调汁师
12. Kitchen Clerk	l. 头粘
13. Dim Sum Fryer	m. 二粘
14. Steamer	n. 烧烤厨师

Activity 2

Read the following Chinese words in column A and try to match them with the English versions in column B.

A	B
1. 总厨	a. General Cook
2. 点心总厨	b. Service Cook
3. 二厨	c. Senior Cook
4. 三厨	d. Vegetable Cook
5. 四厨	e. Junior Cook
6. 西厨	f. Dim Sum Cook
7. 糕饼师傅	g. Pastry Cook
8. 点心厨师	h. Cook (Western)
9. 见习厨师	i. No. 4 Cook
10. 蔬菜厨师	j. No. 2 Cook
11. 高级厨师	k. No. 3 Cook

12. 打荷
13. 普通厨师
14. 烧烤厨师

l. Chief Cook
m. Chief Dim Sum Cook
n. Barbecue Cook

Activity 3

Listen to the following passage and write the points according to the requirements.

Storage Areas for Food
The Function of the Storage Areas
Items Stored in the Dry Storage Areas
Temperature in the Storeroom

Learning Tips

Food Protection

The major sanitation problem will be food-borne (*adj.* 食物传染的) illnesses. The reasons can be the following: inadequate cooling and cold holding; preparing food ahead of planned service; poor personal hygiene (*n.* 卫生); infected persons; inadequate cleaning of equipment; cross-contamination (*n.* 污染); inadequate cooking or heat processing, etc. The Hazard Analysis Critical Control Points (HACCP) system, developed in the 1960s to ensure the safety of food prepared for astronauts, is set up to maximize food safety. The system combines three elements—principles of food microbiology (*n.* 微生物学), quality control, and risk assessment. And it emphasizes a movement away from the inspection of facilities to one that centers on the process of preparing and serving safe food.

Part B Tools and Utensils for Food Production

Teaching hours: 2 hours

LEARNING GOALS

To be able to
* get familiar with the equipment and utensils for baking, frying, roasting, grilling/broiling, etc.
* know different tools for preparing meat, fish, vegetables, fruits, etc.
* know different knives and scissors for preparing meat, fish, etc.

VOCABULARY ASSISTANCE

skewer/brochette	n.	串肉扦	mixing bowl		调拌钵
mallet	n.	木槌	cake tin/pan		蛋糕烤盘
steel	n.	磨刀用的工具	loaf tin/pan		面包斗
spatula	n.	刮铲, 抹刀	cooling tray/rack		降温盘
scaler	n.	去鱼鳞器	pie dish		馅饼盘
grill	n.	炙烤架	bun tin/Muffin pan		松饼烤盘
wok	n.	炒菜锅	rolling pin		擀面杖
casserole	n.	炖锅	frying pan		有柄煎锅
cleaver	n.	切肉的大菜刀	pressure cooker		高压锅
saucepan	n.	深平底锅	potato masher		土豆捣烂器
chopper	n.	屠刀, 大砍刀	cutlet bat		肉片, 鱼片拍板
steamer	n.	蒸锅	pallet knife		铲刀
sieve	n.	筛子	paring knife		水果刀
bicarbonate	n.	碳酸氢盐	grapefruit knife		西柚刀
salami	n.	意大利蒜味香肠	fish scissors		鱼剪刀
trim	v.	整理, 修剪	poultry shears		家禽拔毛剪
split	v.	切开	kitchen cutters		厨房刀具
strainer	n.	滤器, 滤网	oyster knife		开牡蛎刀
sprinkle (with)	v.	把……撒在……上	boning knife		去骨刀
garnish (with)	v.	给……配上	carving knife		雕刻刀
cheese knife		切奶酪刀	carving set		一套切肉用具

Start You Off

Activity 1

Look at the following pictures and find out the names for these tools.

1._____ 2._____ 3._____

4._____ 5._____ 6._____

7._____ 8._____ 9._____

Activity 2

Look at the pictures below and find out the right words in the box to match them.

| slotted spoon | colander | melon scoop | ladle | pizza cutter |
| butter cutlery | peeler | apple corer | whisk/egg beater | |

1._____ 2._____ 3._____

Unit 2

4. _____ 5. _____ 6. _____

 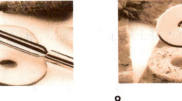 

7. _____ 8. _____ 9. _____

Activity 3

Look at the pictures and find out the names for these tools.

1. _____ 2. _____

3. _____ 4. _____

Focus on Language

Conversation

Read the conversation, answer the questions and practise in pairs.

Baked Fish with Sesame Oil

Commis: What shall I do with this fish?

Chef: Scale it, cut off the fins and then gut it.

Commis: What kind of knife can I use to scale the fish?

Chef: Use the fish scaler to do it. And use these fish scissors to gut it.

Commis: So these are special scissors.

Chef: Yes. Use them to cut open the stomach of the fish. Then take out the guts.

Commis: OK.

Chef: After you finish it, cook some onion.

Commis: I already did.

Chef: Then mix the sesame seed, water, garlic, salt, lemon juice and red pepper with the spoon.

Commis: All right. What next?

Chef: Sprinkle the baking dish with breadcrumbs and parsley.

Commis: Shall I put the fish in the baking dish?

Chef: Yes. Pour the sesame seed and onions over the fish. Light the oven and cook the fish at 400 degrees.

Commis: For how long?

Chef: For twenty or twenty-five minutes. When it is cooked, garnish the fish with parsley and olives.

Questions:

1. What will the commis do with the fish?
2. What kind of tools does the commis use to scale and gut the fish?
3. How many ingredients are there in this dish?
4. Where does the commis put the fish?
5. What does the chef ask the commis to pour over the fish?
6. For how long do they cook the fish?

Language Tips

1. The equipment and utensils for baking, frying, roasting, grilling/broiling, etc.

Practice 1

Look at the pictures given below. Work in pairs and try to learn the proper names in English.

1. mixing bowl

2. cake tin/pan

3. loaf tin/pan

Unit 2

4. cooling tray/rack

5. pie dish

6. bun tin/muffin pan

7. pastry

8. flour

9. rolling pin

Practice 2

Look at the pictures given in Practice 1. Work in pairs and try to find out the proper things you are going to use when you want to bake cakes, muffin, bread and pie.

Cakes: _____
Muffin: _____
Bread: _____
Pie: _____

Practice 3

Work in groups. Try to figure out what they are in the following pictures and try to tell what they are used for according to the model given below.

1. frying pan

Description:
Frying Pan is used to fry meat, fish, eggs, etc.

2. _____

Description:
_____
_____
_____
_____

3. _____

Description:
_____
_____
_____
_____

4. _____

Description:
_____
_____
_____
_____

5. _____

Description:
_____
_____
_____
_____

6. _____

Description:
_____
_____
_____
_____

7. _____

Description:
_____
_____
_____
_____

8. _____

Description:
_____
_____
_____
_____

Unit 2

2. Different tools for preparing meat, fish, vegetables, fruits, etc.

Practice

Look at the pictures and find out their names in English. Then complete the short conversations according to the example given below.

Example:

A. What do you call this?
B. It's a **whisk**.
A. What are you going to do with it?
B. I'm going to **beat eggs** with it.

1. _____

A. What do you call this?
B. It's a _____.
A. What are you going to do with it?
B. I'm going to _____ with it.

2. _____

A. What do you call this?
B. It's a _____.
A. What are you going to do with it?
B. I'm going to _____ with it.

3. _____

A. What do you call this?
B. It's a _____.
A. What are you going to do with it?
B. I'm going to _____ with it.

4. _____

A. What do you call this?
B. It's a _____.
A. What are you going to do with it?
B. I'm going to _____ with it.

5. _____

A. What do you call this?
B. It's a _____.
A. What are you going to do with it?
B. I'm going to _____ with it.

6. _____

A. What do you call this?
B. It's a _____.
A. What are you going to do with it?
B. I'm going to _____ with it.

7. _____

A. What do you call this?
B. It's a _____.
A. What are you going to do with it?
B. I'm going to _____ with it.

8. _____

A. What do you call this?
B. It's a _____.
A. What are you going to do with it?
B. I'm going to _____ with it.

3. **Different knives and scissors for preparing meat, fish, vegetables, fruits, etc.**

Practice

Look at the pictures and find out their names in English. Then complete the following short conversations in pairs.

Example:

A. What do you call this?
B. It's a whisk.
A. What are you going to do with it?
B. I'm going to beat eggs with it.

Unit 2

1. _____

A. What do you call this?
B. _____
A. What are you going to do with it?
B. _____

2. _____

A. What do you call this?
B. _____
A. What are you going to do with it?
B. _____

3. _____

A. What do you call this?
B. _____
A. What are you going to do with it?
B. _____

4. _____

A. What do you call this?
B. _____
A. What are you going to do with it?
B. _____

5. _____

A. What do you call this?
B. _____
A. What are you going to do with it?
B. _____

6. _____

A. What do you call this?
B. _____
A. What are you going to do with it?
B. _____

7. _____

A. What do you call this?
B. _____
A. What are you going to do with it?
B. _____

8. _____

A. What do you call this?
B. _____
A. What are you going to do with it?
B. _____

9. _____

A. What do you call this?
B. _____
A. What are you going to do with it?
B. _____

10. _____

A. What do you call this?
B. _____
A. What are you going to do with it?
B. _____

Summarize Key Expressions

1. **The equipment and utensils for baking, frying, roasting, grilling/broiling, etc.**

   a. mixing bowl
   b. cake tin/pan
   c. loaf tin/pan
   d. cooling tray/rack
   e. pie dish
   f. bun tin/muffin pan
   g. rolling pin
   h. frying pan
   i. pressure cooker
   j. top fry/grill
   k. oven
   l. wok
   m. casserole
   n. saucepan
   o. steamer
   p. stew pan
   q. oval pan
   r. charlotte cake pan
   s. asparagus kettle
   t. soup pot

u. egg poacher
v. double boiler
w. griddle
x. pot

2. **Different tools for preparing meat, fish, vegetables, fruits, etc.**

   a. potato masher
   b. sieve
   c. cutlet bat
   d. skewer/brochette
   e. mallet
   f. steel
   g. spatula
   h. fish scale
   i. apple corer
   j. peeler
   k. jar opener
   l. tin/can opener
   m. bottle opener
   n. corkscrew
   o. grater
   p. garlic press
   q. mortar
   r. grinder
   s. ice cream portioner
   t. lemon squeezer/ juicer
   u. nutcracker
   v. whisk/egg beater
   w. measuring cup
   x. strainer
   y. roasting fork
   z. egg slicer

3. **Different knives and scissors for preparing meat, fish, vegetables, fruits, etc.**

   a. pallet knife
   b. paring knife
   c. grapefruit knife
   d. steak knife
   e. fish scissors
   f. poultry shears
   g. kitchen cutters
   h. cleaver
   i. chopper
   j. oyster knife
   k. boning knife
   l. carving knife
   m. cheese knife
   n. carving set
   o. bone saw
   p. electric bone saw

Give It a Try

Task 1

Listen to the following short conversations and write down the answers to what the Vegetable Chef is asking the Commis Cook to do.

Conversation 1
The Vegetable Chef is asking the Commis Cook to:

➤ _____
➤ _____
➤ _____

► _____
► _____
► _____

Conversation 2

The Vegetable Chef is asking the Commis Cook to:

► _____
► _____
► _____
► _____
► _____
► _____

Conversation 3

The Vegetable Chef is asking the Commis Cook to:

► _____
► _____
► _____
► _____
► _____

Conversation 4

The Vegetable Chef is asking the Commis Cook to:

► _____
► _____
► _____
► _____
► _____
► _____

Task 2

Read the statements given below and rearrange them into the proper steps for preparing and cooking the dishes.

1. Cooking the cabbage
   a. Stuff the cabbage.
   b. Add bicarbonate to the water.
   c. Boil the cabbage.
   d. Cut each head of cabbage in half.

2. Preparing the tomatoes for tomato soup
   a. Put the tomatoes in boiling water for fifteen seconds.
   b. Peel the tomatoes easily.
   c. Wash the tomatoes.
   d. Put them immediately in ice cold water.
   e. Cut out the centers of the tomatoes.
3. Preparing carrots
   a. Boil the carrots in salt water.
   b. Wash the carrots carefully.
   c. Cut the carrots into batons.
   d. Serve the carrots with butter.
   e. Peel the carrots.
4. Cooking green peppers
   a. Cut the green peppers open.
   b. Cook the green peppers in tomato sauce.
   c. Stuff the green peppers with meat.
   d. Remove the seeds.
   e. Wash the green peppers.

Task 3

Listen to the following conversation and complete the chart below with the proper names of different knives for preparing food and their functions according to the recording.

The Names of Different Knives	The Functions of the Knives

Task 4

Work in pairs. Make short conversations according to the situations given below.

Example:

Commis: What do you call this tray?

Chef: It's a roasting tray.

Commis: What are you going to do with it?

Chef: I'm going to heat oil in it.

Commis: And then?

Chef: We'll roast chicken.

Commis: I see. And what shall I do?

Chef: Put the roasting tray in the oven.
Commis: OK.

Situations:

a. To fry potatoes in a sauté pan.
b. To make a stew.
c. To mince or grind meat.
d. To use a machine to slice things.

Do Extension Activities

Activity 1

There are many different ways of preparing and cooking food. Take mushrooms, for example. They can be fried—fried mushrooms, grilled—grilled mushrooms, or deep-fried—deep-fried mushrooms. Now work in groups and use the illustrations given below to decide how the various foods can be prepared. Then try to give the description.

Example:
Mushroom: a, c, f

Ways of preparing and cooking food:

a. frying

b. boiling

c. grilling

d. roasting/baking

e. poaching

f. deep-frying

Unit 2

Food for cooking:

1. duck

2. T-bone steak

3. bread

4. eggs

5. potatoes

6. chicken

7. bacon

8. salmon

9. leg of lamb

Activity 2

Make a discussion in groups and try to describe how to cook or prepare the following food.

1. How do you make French fries? (炸薯条)

Description:
_____
_____
_____

2. How do you make mayonnaise? (蛋黄酱)

Description:
_____
_____
_____

3. How do you roast meat? (盘烤肉)

   Description:
   _____
   _____
   _____

4. How do you braise beef? (炖牛肉)

   Description:
   _____
   _____
   _____

Activity 3

Group work. Follow the directions given below and make Tuna Fish Salad after class.

Directions:

1. Cut the green peppers in half, cutting lengthwise from top to bottom. Place the green peppers, skin facing up, under a hot grill until soft. Skin the green peppers and cut them into thin strips.
2. Slice off the tops of the tomatoes and scoop out the seeds. Cut the tomatoes into rings. Chop finely the spring onions and chili peppers.
3. Put all the vegetables into a bowl. Drain the can of tuna and then add the fish to the salad. Arrange the sliced eggs on top and sprinkle the salad with capers.
4. Mix all the ingredients for the dressing and pour it over the salad. Garnish the salad with parsley.

Learning Tips

Being a Service Person Is a Demanding Job

Being a service person is a demanding job. Employees should look and smell clean because cleanliness would create the atmosphere that guests are looking for. Male employees cannot have any facial hair, nor can their hair length be touching their costume collar. Females cannot wear long, dangling earrings. The acceptable size of earrings is the size of a dime. Nail polish is limited to a clear color. Kitchen staff should wear hair covers to avoid hair falling into food items. If your guests are waited on by a person with dirty, scuffed shoes, they may think that the cook is not clean. To the guests, the service person is the restaurant.

Unit 3

Condiments

Part A Sauce, Paste & Powdered Condiments

Teaching hours: 2 hours

LEARNING GOALS

To be able to
- get familiar with condiments
- know the English names of condiments
- know how to classify condiments
- talk about the taste of condiments

VOCABULARY ASSISTANCE

condiment	n.	调味品		ketchup	n.	番茄酱
mustard	n.	芥末		spicy	adj.	香的,辛辣的
vinegar	n.	醋		sour	adj.	酸的
salt	n.	盐		salty	adj.	咸的
spread	v.	涂抹食品		ingredient	n.	成分
wasabi	n.	青芥末		onion	n.	洋葱
edible	adj.	可以吃的		fermented	adj.	发酵的
hot	adj.	辣的		sugar	n.	糖
sweet	adj	甜的		ginger	n.	姜
chutney	n.	酸辣调味品		cucumber	n.	黄瓜
slice	n.	片,薄片		dice	n.	小方块
honey	n.	蜂蜜		dressing	n.	加味品
major	adj.	主要的		beverage	n.	饮料
topping	n.	(食品上面的)配品		jam	n.	果酱
jelly	n.	果子冻,肉冻		marmalade	n.	橘子酱
roll	n	面包卷,卷饼		pancake	n.	薄煎饼
category	n.	种类,类		shaker	n.	调味瓶
coarse	adj.	粗的,粗糙的		consumption	n.	消费,使用
preservative	n.	防腐剂				

versatile	adj.	通用的，多方面适用的	horse-radish	n.	辣根
curry powder		咖喱	tomato sauce		番茄酱
soy sauce		酱油	chili paste		辣酱
rock sugar		冰糖	Worcestershire sauce		辣椒油
soybean paste		黄酱	maple syrup		枫叶糖浆，汁
chili pepper		红辣椒			

Start You Off

Activity 1

Look at the pictures below and tell what they are.

Activity 2

Look at the pictures below and match the words with the pictures.

Unit 3

1. wasabi 2. salt & pepper 3. soy sauce
4. tomato sauce 5. syrup 6. chili paste

Focus on Language

Listen to the tape and decide whether the following statements are true or false.

1. Condiment is a substance or mixture that makes the food more tasty.
2. Condiment is not eatable.
3. Condiments are often placed in the cupboard for the convenience of the diners.
4. There are different kinds of condiments.

⇨ Language Tips

1. Classifying condiments

◆ What is condiment?
◇ Condiment is a substance that gives the food a strong flavor.
◆ How many kinds of condiments are there?
◇ There are salty, sweet, spicy, pickled condiments, compound sauces and so on.

Practice 1

Listen to the tape and answer the following questions.

1. What is the earliest condiment employed by humans?
2. What do people use salt for?
3. What are the other usages of salt?

Practice 2

Listen to the tape and complete the following statements.

1. Sugar or other sweeteners are _____.
2. Sweet condiments include _____.
3. Sugar and honey are used _____.
4. They are also used _____.
5. Maple syrup is commonly used _____.

2. Talking about the flavor of condiments

◆ What is it?
◇ It is vinegar.
◆ Is it sweet?
◇ No, it is sour.

Practice 1

Look at the pictures below and make similar conversations as the example given above.

Practice 2

Match the words in column A with the words in column B.

A	B
1. spicy and hot	a. 咸
2. sour	b. 苦
3. sweet	c. 辣
4. bitter	d. 酸
5. salty	e. 甜

Practice 3

Look up the following words of condiments in the dictionary and tell their taste.

honey   garlic   maple syrup   chili pepper
ginger   soybean paste   rock sugar

Summarize Key Expressions

1. **Classifying condiments**
   a. How many types/ kinds of condiments are there?
   There are altogether 5 types of condiments.
   b. What are the types of condiments?
   They are salty, sweet, spicy, pickled condiments, compound sauces and so on.
   c. How many categories of condiments are there?
   Condiments fall into five categories.

2. **Talking about the flavor of condiments**
   a. What is the flavor/ taste of it?
   It is sour/ salty/ too hot/ bitter/ sweet.
   b. Is it sweet or salty?
   It is sweet.
   c. It is hot and spicy, isn't it?
   Yes, it is./ Yes, you are right.
   d. Does it taste good?
   It tastes good/ bad/ terrible.

Give It a Try

Task 1

Listen to the tape and answer the following questions.

1. When did people begin to have pickled condiments?
2. What do common pickled foods used as condiments include?
3. How are the pickled condiments served?

Task 2

Listen to the tape and fill in the blanks.

　　A _____ condiment category are those _____ or hot foods, such as _____ pepper, _____ pepper, mustard, _____, horse-radish and _____. A product of _____, black pepper is commonly _____ from shakers throughout the _____ world in a dried state and is _____ ground into coarse or fine state _____ consumption.

Do Extension Activities

Activity 1

Listen to the tape and write out the missing information.

1. Compound sauces include: _____
   _____
   _____
   _____
   _____
   _____
   _____

2. The earliest known compound sauces made of fish were well accepted
   in _____ and _____.

Activity 2

Listen to the information of Russian Mustard and write it down.

Russian Mustard: _____
_____
_____
_____

Activity 3

The following are some condiments used in Chinese cuisine. Match the words in English with those in Chinese.

cinnamon, sesame oil, sugar, chili sauce, mustard, honey, gourmet powder, oyster oil, salt, soy sauce, vinegar, ketchup, pepper, curry

| 盐 | 糖 | 香油 | 蚝油 | 酱油 | 醋 | 番茄酱 |
| 辣酱 | 胡椒 | 桂皮 | 蜂蜜 | 咖喱 | 芥末 | 味精 |

Activity 4

Listen to the conversation and write out the missing information.

1. There are _____ different condiments mentioned in this conversation.
   They are Worcestershire sauce, v_____, t_____ paste, c_____ and m_____.

2. Vinegar has a big variety. _____ different vinegars are often used in western cuisine. They are:

balsamic vinegar	意大利香脂醋	champagne vinegar	香槟酒醋
_____ vinegar	香草醋	tarragon vinegar	他里根香醋
malt vinegar	麦芽醋	_____ vinegar	葡萄酒醋
sherry vinegar	雪利酒醋	_____ vinegar	苹果醋
aromatic vinegar	醋精	and _____ vinegar	白醋

Activity 5

Listen to the conversation again and repeat it.

Learning Tips

Condiment

The term "condiment" originally meant seasoned, pickled, or preserved foods in Latin. Today, the word is broadly applied to a variety of foods, including spices, herbs, sauces, seasonings, flavorings, colorings, and even beverages, such as tea, coffee, and alcoholic drinks. A more narrow definition is that a condiment is a substance added to other foods for the purpose of giving a strong flavor. Condiments usually appear on the table and are intended for individual use by the diner.

Part B Spices

Teaching hours: 2 hours

LEARNING GOALS

To be able to
* get familiar with spices
* know the English names of spices
* tell the culinary uses of spices
* tell the flavor of different spices
* know the places of production of species

VOCABULARY ASSISTANCE

spice	n.	香料	rhizomes	n.	根茎
bark	n.	茎皮	seed	adj.	种子
nutmeg	n.	肉豆蔻	India	n.	印度
appropriate	adj.	合适的,恰当的	ground	adj.	(grind 的过去分词)磨碎的
add	v.	加入	seasoning	n.	佐料
process	n.	过程	culinary	adj.	烹饪的
preserve	v.	保持	aroma	n.	香味
cloves	n.	丁香	pungent	adj.	刺鼻的,辣的
aromatic	adj.	芳香的,有香味的	cinnamon	n.	桂皮
saffron	n.	番红花	nutty	adj.	有坚果味的
aprika	n.	甜椒粉	oregano	n.	牛至
betelnut	n.	槟榔	mainly	adv.	主要地
produce	v.	生产	Hungary	n.	匈牙利
originate	v.	发源	Europe	n.	欧洲
Asia	n.	亚洲	Indonesia	n.	印度尼西亚
chief	adj.	主要的	madeira	n.	(玛德拉岛产的)白葡萄酒
fiery	adj.	火热的,火辣的	mild	adj.	味淡的
fresh	adj.	新鲜的	brandy	n.	白兰地
whisky	n.	威士忌	gin	n.	金酒
rhum	n.	朗姆酒	champagne	n.	香槟酒
anisette	n.	茴香酒	sherry	n.	雪利酒
places of production		产地	red wine		红葡萄酒

54

port wine	钵酒	bay leaf	香叶
the Philippines	菲律宾	white wine	白葡萄酒

Start You Off

Activity 1

Look at the pictures below and tell what they are.

Activity 2

Look at the pictures and match the words with the pictures.

cinnamon 桂皮   thyme 百里香   cloves 丁香
nutmeg 肉豆蔻   betelnut 槟榔   saffron 番红花

Focus on Language

Listen to the tape and fill in the blanks.

Spices

There are about 35 spices which can be broadly classified into 6 groups, based upon the _____ of the _____ which they are obtained, namely (i) rhizomes and _____ spices, (ii) _____ spices, (iii) _____ spices, (iv) _____ spices, (v) _____ spices, and (vi) _____ spices.

➪ Language Tips

1. Discussing the culinary uses of spices

◆ What is this?
◇ This is bay leaf.
◆ What is the culinary use of it?
◇ It is used as seasoning and so on.

Practice 1

Listen to the tape and answer the following questions.

1. What is bay leaf?
2. What is it used for?
3. What is it often included as?

Practice 2

Listen to the tape and answer the following questions.

1. How many kinds of peppers are mentioned on the tape? What are they?
2. What is the best way of using pepper?
3. Why is white pepper rather than black pepper used in white sauces?
4. How are green peppercorns used?

Practice 3

Pair work: Make a conversation talking about the culinary use of bay leaf and pepper.

2. Talking about the flavor of spices

◆ Have you ever heard of bay leaf?
◇ Of course. It's a kind of spices.
◆ What's the flavor of it?
◇ It is slightly bitter and strongly aromatic.

Practice 1

Listen to the tape, write out the flavor of the following spices and make similar conversations as the example given above.

> nutmeg   cloves   cinnamon

56

Practice 2

Listen to the tape and decide whether the following statements are true or false.

Black pepper is less pungent.
White pepper is very pungent and fiery.
Green pepper is milder with a cleaner, fresher flavor.

Practice 3

Make conversations talking about the flavor of peppers, nutmeg, cloves and cinnamon within the speaking pairs.

Summarize Key Expressions

1. Discussing the culinary uses of spices

   a. Can you tell me the best culinary use of pepper?
      Pepper is best ground directly onto food.
   b. What is the best use of bay leaf?
      Bay leaf may be best used in soups, sauces, stews and it is an appropriate seasoning for fish, meat and poultry.
   c. What is the proper amount of ground cloves to be used in cooking dishes?
      Ground cloves are stronger than whole ones, so take care to use only a pinch otherwise the flavor will be too overpowering.

2. Talking about the flavor of spices

   a. What is the flavor of pepper?
      Black pepper is very pungent and fiery. White pepper is less pungent and green pepper is milder with a cleaner, fresher flavor.
   b. Is nutmeg nutty?
      It is not only nutty, but also warm and slightly sweet.
   c. Cloves are aromatic, aren't they?
      Yes, they are strongly aromatic.

Give It a Try

Task 1

Listen to the tape and fill in the blanks.

Cinnamon

Cinnamon is used _____ in dessert dishes. It is commonly used in _____ and other _____ goods, milk and rice _____, chocolate dishes and _____ desserts, particularly _____ and _____. It is common in many _____ and _____ dishes. Cinnamon is used in flavoring _____.

Task 2

Listen to the same tape again and make a conversation talking about the culinary use of cinnamon.

Do Extension Activities

Activity 1

Listen to the tape and write out the kind of meat and vegetables working well with thyme.

Meat	Vegetables	
v _ _ _	t _ _ _ _ _ _ _	a _ _ _ _ _ _ _ _
l _ _ _	o _ _ _ _ _	g _ _ _ _ _ _ _ _ _
b _ _ _	c _ _ _ _ _ _ _ _	b _ _ _ _ _ _ _
p _ _ _ _ _ _	c _ _ _ _ _ _	s _ _ _ _ _ _ _ _ _
f _ _ _	e _ _ _ _ _ _ _	p _ _ _ _ _ _ _
	l _ _ _ _	s _ _ _ _ _ _ _
	m _ _ _ _ _ _ _ _	p _ _ _

Listen to the tape again and speak out what else work well with thyme.

_____ _____ _____ _____ _____
_____ _____ _____

Activity 2

Listen to the tape and match the words in column A with those in column B and in column C.

A	B	C
aprika	slightly bitter & strongly aromatic	Europe, West and South Asia
oregano	slightly sweet	Indonesia, the Philippines, India
betelnut	bitter and strongly aromatic	Hungary

Activity 3

Listen to the tape and write out the missing information.

The basic classification of spices is as follows: First, _____, for example, bay leaf, tarragon(茵陈嵩), thyme(百里香), oregano. Second,_____. Examples include fennel(茴香), coriander(香菜), mustard(芥末), black pepper etc. Third, _____. Examples include garlic, onion, celery and ginger.

Activity 4

Read the passage and do the following exercises.

Classification and Types of Different Spices

Basil(罗勒叶) is most commonly recommended to be used fresh. In cooked recipes it is generally added at the last moment, because cooking quickly destroys the flavor. Basil can be kept for a short time in plastic bags in the refrigerator, or for a longer period in the freezer, after being blanched(焯)quickly in boiling water. The dried Basil also loses most of its flavor, and what little flavor remains tastes very differently. Chinese use fresh or dried basils in soups and other foods. In Taiwan, people add fresh basil leaves into thick soups.

Hyssop(牛膝草)is native from the Mediterranean east to central Asia. They are aromatic. Hyssop leaves have slightly bitter mint flavor and can be added to soups, salads or meats, although should be used sparingly(节约的, 少量的) as the flavor is very strong.

Saffron is often dried and used in cooking as a seasoning and coloring. Saffron, which has for decades been the world's most expensive spice by weight, is native to Asia. Saffron's taste is somewhat bitter. It contributes a yellow-orange coloring to foods. It is widely used in Iranian, Arab, Central Asia, European, Indian and Turkish cuisines.

Many egg, fish and other dishes employ fresh or dried fennel leaves. Florence fennel is a key ingredient in some Italian and German salads.

Chives(小香葱), native to Europe, Asia and North America, are the smallest species of the onion family. Chives have a wide variety of culinary uses, such as in traditional France and Sweden dishes or used as condiment for fish, pancakes, potatoes and soups.

Sage (鼠尾草) is native to the Mediterranean region. It has a slight peppery flavor. In Western cooking, it is used for flavoring fatty meats and some drinks. In the United States and Britain, sage is used with onion for poultry or pork stuffing and also in sauces. In French cuisine, sage is used for cooking white meat and in vegetable soups. Germans often use it in sausage dishes, and sage forms the dominant flavoring in the English Lincolnshire sausage. Sage is also common in Italian cooking. In the Middle East, it is used when roasting mutton.

I. Read the passage and decide whether the following statements are True or False.

1. Basil is suggested to be used fresh.
2. The more Hyssop leaves used, the better flavor we have.
3. Saffron has been used greatly in Asian and European cuisines.
4. Florence fennel is very important in some Italian cooking.
5. In traditional France and Sweden dishes, Chives have been widely used.
6. Sage is not used in the English Lincolnshire sausage.

II. Answer the following questions.

1. When is the proper time for Basil to be used in cooked recipes? Why?
2. What are the ways of preserving Basil?
3. How many Hyssop leaves can be used in soups, salads or meats? Why?
4. How and where is Saffron used?
5. What is special with Chives?
6. In cooking what is Sage widely sued?
7. Which spice tastes bitter?

III. Match the words in column A with the statements in column B.

A	B
chives	contributing a yellow-orange coloring to foods
fennel leaves	often used in cooking meat and vegetable soups
sage	widely used as condiments for fish, pancakes, potatoes and soups
saffron	often used in egg, fish and other dishes

Learning Tips

Brandy, whisky, gin, rum, red wine, white wine, champagne, sherry, madeira, anisette, port wine which could help to get rid of the unpleasant smell are often used as condiments when cooking, especially when meat or fish are cooked.

Unit 4

Food Material I

Part A BOM

Teaching hours: 2 hours

LEARNING GOALS

To be able to
* know the English names of vegetables
* describe vegetables in English
* know some information about vegetables
* express likes and dislikes of vegetables

VOCABULARY ASSISTANCE

calcium	n.	钙		nutrition	n.	营养
purple	adj.	紫色的		crispness	n.	脆
diet	n.	饮食		pumpkin	n.	南瓜
eggplant	n.	茄子		hardy	adj.	坚硬的
characteristic	adj.	典型的		bruising	n.	硬伤
store	v.	存放		decay	n.	腐烂
calorie	n.	卡路里(热量单位)		fiber	n.	纤维
protein	n.	蛋白质		light yellow		浅黄色
carbohydrate	n.	碳水化合物		trim off		修剪
deterioration	n.	恶化		dark green		深绿色
investment	n.	投资,投入				

Start You Off

Activity 1

Can you name these fruits in English? Try to match the pictures with the words in the box.

potato	carrot	bean	broccoli	celery	circumber
onion	lettuce	pea	tomato	Chinese cabbage	
pumpkin	eggplant (aubergine)		cauliflower	capsicum	

Chinese cabbage

_____

_____

_____

_____

_____

_____

_____

_____

_____

_____

_____

Unit 4

_____   _____   _____

Activity 2

What colors are they? Try to name the following colors in English.

红色   蓝色   黄色   黑色
red   _____   _____   _____

绿色   白色   紫色   棕色
_____   _____   _____   _____

深绿色   浅黄色   灰色   橙色
_____   _____   _____   _____

Ask each other the questions, following the example.

Example:

A: What is the color of the Chinese cabbage?
B: It's white.
A: Do you like it?
B: Yes, I do. / No, I don't.
A: Why / Why not?
B: ...

Focus on Language

How to Choose Vegetables

Questions:

1. What kind of vegetables are fresh?
2. Do you know how to choose vegetables when you buy them?
3. Do you know how to store vegetables?

Demand freshness! Check the characteristic signs of freshness such as bright, lively color and crispness. Vegetables are usually at their best quality and price at the peak of their season.

Use thoughtful care to prevent injury to vegetables. Some vegetables are more hardy than others, but bruising and damage can be prevented by just being careful. The consumer pays for carelessness in the long run.

Don't buy because of low price alone. It doesn't pay to buy more vegetables than you can properly store in your refrigerator or use without waste. Most fresh vegetables can be stored for 2 to 5 days, except for root vegetables, which can be stored from one to several weeks.

Avoid decay. It's a waste of money to buy fresh vegetables affected by decay. Even if you do trim off the decayed area, rapid deterioration is likely to spread to other areas. Paying a few cents extra for vegetables in good condition is a good investment.

Vegetables are important to people's health. They contain calories, protein, carbohydrate and fiber. They are also an excellent source of Vitamin A and Vitamin C.

Language Tips

1. Methods of choosing vegetables

◆ Demand …
◇ Check …
◆ Use thoughtful care to do ….
◇ Avoid …
◆ It's a waste of money to …
◇ … be likely to …
◆ … because of …

Practice 1

What kind of vocabulary have you learned from the passage? Write the words for:

Fresh vegetables	Bad vegetables

Practice 2

Complete the sentences with the information you've got from the passage.

1. When you buy vegetables, the most important thing you need to consider is _____ .
2. The characteristic signs of freshness are _____ .
3. Vegetables are usually at their _____ at the peak of their season.
4. You should be very careful to _____ to vegetables.
5. The consumer pays for _____ in the long run.
6. It isn't a good idea to buy vegetables of _____ .
7. Don't buy _____ vegetables than you can properly store in your refrigerator.
8. _____ vegetables can be stored for more than one week.
9. It's a waste of money to buy fresh vegetables _____ .
10. Even if you cut off the decayed area, _____ is likely to spread to other areas.

Practice 3

Answer the following questions.

1. What is important when you choose vegetables?
2. How can you tell whether the vegetable is fresh?
3. When are vegetables at their best quality?
4. How can you prevent injury to vegetables?
5. Is it a good idea to buy more vegetables because of low price? Why? Why not?
6. How long can most of the vegetables be stored?
7. What should you avoid when you buy vegetables? Why?

Summarize Key Expressions

1. **Vegetables are usually at their best quality and price at the peak of their season.**
2. **Use thoughtful care to prevent injury to vegetables.**
3. **The consumer pays for carelessness in the long run.**
4. **Don't buy because of low price alone.**
5. **Avoid decay.**
6. **Paying a few cents extra for vegetables in good condition is a good investment.**

Give It a Try

Task 1

Complete the sentences using these words. Change the form if necessary.

| cucumber | celery | cabbage | carrot | tomato |
| pumpkin | cauliflower | capsicum | eggplant | leek |

1. The name _____ developed in the United States, Australia, New Zealand and Canada because the fruits of some 18th century European cultivars were yellow or white and resembled goose or hens while the name aubergine in British English developed based on the French *aubergine*.

2. _____ are a fruit, but they are served and prepared as a vegetable. That is why most people consider them a vegetable and not a fruit.

3. _____ used to be the main vegetable in winter for people in Beijing in 1960s and 1970s.

4. _____ is a member of the onion family, but the taste is milder than either onion or garlic. Many people like to make dumplings with it.

5. _____ are a root vegetable deep orange to red in color. They should be medium sized, firm, smooth and well formed.

6. The head of the _____ is surrounded by crisp, bluish-green leaves. The head should be firm, compact and creamy white with florets pressed tightly together.

7. Depending on the variety, it may be mild, sweet, hot or fiery. _____ are also called green, red or yellow peppers.

8. People in western countries like to decorate _____ on Halloween.

9. There is a common belief that _____ is so difficult for humans to digest. However, it is very valuable in diets, where it provides low calorie.

10. _____ are grown to either be eaten fresh or to be pickled.

Task 2

Translate the words in brackets to complete the sentences.

1. All the vegetables _____ (要求) your thoughtful care.
2. What can we do to _____ (避免) the decay spreading?
3. When you buy vegetables, _____ (检查) whether the vegetables are fresh.
4. The boy _____ (躲避) punishment by running away.
5. Don't buy too many vegetables at one time _____ (因为) the low price.
6. The decayed vegetables _____ (很有可能) affect the good ones.

Task 3

Work in groups of four and ask each other what kind of vegetables you like, and why.

Task 4

Contest: Divide the class into two groups and ask students of each group to write as many vegetables in English as possible on the blackboard. The group that writes more vegetables is the winner.

Do Extension Activities

Activity 1

In each of the following groups, three words collocate with the word on the right. Which is the odd one out in each group?

1. fast
   junk   food
   easy
   frozen
2. simple
   plain   food
   rich
   fat
3. strong
   hard   flavour
   mild
   distinctive
4. healthy
   fit   food
   organic
   fresh
5. main
   light   meal
   heavy
   fast
6. thin
   healthy   diet
   balanced
   fat-free

Activity 2

Crossword Puzzle: Work with your partner and complete the table below.

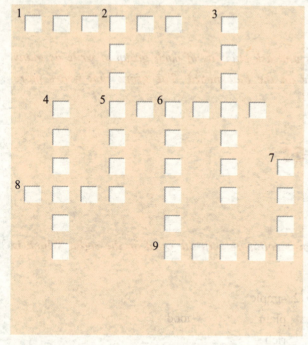

Across

1. Some are used to make hot sauce. Some aren't hot at all.
5. You can bake, mash or fry it.
8. Soy _____ is widely cultivated for its nutritious seeds.
9. You often cry when you cut it.

Down

2. You make a Jack-o'-Lantern with this vegetable.
3. It's a green leaf used in salads and hamburgers.
4. It's a high-fiber, stringy stalk, used in soups or salads.
6. You cook it to prepare red sauce.
7. Many people eat _____ flakes for breakfast.

Learning Tips

The History of Potato

Can you imagine the life without French fries? Potatoes are liked today. But in the past this was not true. Potatoes grew in South America five thousand years ago. But they were only eaten in other places two hundred years ago.

In the 16th century, the Spanish brought the potato from South America to Europe. But the people in Europe did not like this strange vegetable. Some people thought that if you ate the potato your skin would look like the skin of a potato. Other people could not believe that you could eat the underground part of the plant. So they ate the leaves instead. This made them sick because there is poison in the leaves. In the 1800s, people started to eat potatoes. In Ireland potatoes became the main food. Then in 1845, a disease killed all the potatoes in Ireland. Two million people died of hunger.

Today each country has its potato dish. Germans eat potato salad, and the United States has the baked potato. And of course the French invented French fries. Now French fries are liked all over the world. The English eat them with salt and vinegar; the French eat them with salt and pepper; and the Ameiricans eat with ketchup.

Unit 4

Part B Vegetable Process

Teaching hours: 2 hours

LEARNING GOALS

To be able to
* know different English terms of processing vegetables
* describe how to process vegetables in English
* be familiar with the expressions of asking for instructions
* be familiar with the expressions of giving proper responses

VOCABULARY ASSISTANCE

sack	n.	袋子,大包	chop	v.	切细,剁碎
fine	adv.	精巧地	brush	n.	刷子
grind	v.	磨(碾)碎	dice	v.	将(菜)切成小块或丁
baton	n.	棍,棒,条状	demonstrate	v.	示范,展示
end	n.	末端,梢,尖	spring onion		生吃的小洋葱,葱

Start You Off

Activity 1

Write the following words under the pictures.

slice   squeeze   beat   grate   peel   chop

69

_____ _____ _____

Activity 2

Match the verbs on the left with the phrases on the right.

1. squeeze   a. the mixture with a wooden spoon
2. melt   b. the potatoes and boil in a pan
3. beat   c. the cheese and add to the sauce
4. mix   d. the sauce over the meat and serve
5. chop   e. the ham as thinly as possible
6. stir   f. the eggs until light and fluffy
7. grate   g. a lemon over the fish
8. slice   h. a little butter in a frying pan
9. pour   i. the vegetables into small pieces
10. peel   j. all the ingredients together

Focus on Language

1. Preparing vegetables

Questions:

1. Do you like cucumbers?
2. What are the ways of eating them?
3. How about cauliflowers? Do you know any good ways of washing them clean?

CONVERSATION 1   **Cucumber**

Commis cook: What shall I do?
Vegetable chef: Get me a couple of fresh cucumbers.
Commis cook: OK. Here they are. What do I do with them?
Vegetable chef: Wash them well.
Commis cook: And peel them then?

Vegetable chef:	That's right.
Commis cook:	And then what?
Vegetable chef:	Slice the cucumbers up.
Commis cook:	For salad?
Vegetable chef:	Yes, for cucumber salad.
Commis cook:	OK.

CONVERSATION 2	**Cauliflower**
Commis cook:	Shall I wash the cauliflower?
Vegetable chef:	Yes. Wash it well.
Commis cook:	Right. Cauliflower is always dirty.
Vegetable chef:	Soak it in salt water.
Commis cook:	For how many minutes?
Vegetable chef:	For thirty minutes.
Commis cook:	And then what?
Vegetable chef:	Split them up into small pieces.
Commis cook:	How shall I cook the cauliflower?
Vegetable chef:	Boil it in water with lemon juice.
Commis cook:	The lemon juice will keep it white.
Vegetable chef:	That's right.

➪ Language Tips

1. Ways of preparing vegetables

- ◆ What shall I do (with the cauliflower)?
- ◇ Shall I wash it?
- ◆ And then what?
- ◇ For how many minutes?
- ◆ How shall I cook it?
- ◇ Get me…
- ◆ Wash it well.
- ◇ Peel them. (Slice them up.)
- ◆ Split them up into small pieces.

Practice 1

Ask your partner the following questions. Suppose you are the commis cook. Try to answer the questions according to the conversations.

1. What shall I do with the cucumbers?

2. What shall I do next?
3. And then what?
4. What shall I do with the cauliflower?
5. Why do I need to wash it well?
6. For how many minutes do I soak it in salt water?
7. What shall I do next?
8. How shall I cook the cauliflower?

Practice 2

Put the following sentences into the correct order according to the time sequence.

1. Split the cauliflower into small pieces.
2. Boil it with lemon juice.
3. Wash the cauliflower.
4. Soak it in salt water.

_____   _____   _____   _____

Practice 3

Complete the following sentences according to the conversations and then read them aloud.

1. What _____ I do?
2. You wash these _____ .
3. And peel _____ .
4. _____ the cucumbers up.
5. We shall _____ the cucumber salad.
6. Shall I _____ the cauliflower?
7. You wash it _____ .
8. Cauliflower is _____ dirty.
9. _____ the cauliflower in salt water.
10. For how _____ minutes?
11. Split the cauliflower into _____ .
12. How _____ I cook the cauliflower?
13. You _____ it in water _____ lemon juice.
14. The lemon juice will _____ it white.

Unit 4

Practice 4

Role-play the conversation between a commis cook and a vegetable chef.

Commis cook: What shall I do with the lettuce?
Vegetable chef: Wash it well.
Commis cook: ...
Vegetable chef: ...

Summarize Key Expressions

Asking for instructions

1. What Shall I Do?

Shall I get a sack of potatoes?
Shall I wash the spring onions?
Shall I trim off the ends of the spring onions?
Shall I scrub the potatoes?
Shall I peel the tomatoes?
Shall I dice the celery?
Shall I grind the garlic?

2. What Do You Need Done?

Do we need onions for the soup?
Do we need it for salad?
Do I need to chop the onions fine?
Do I need to cut the carrots into batons?

3. What Next?

What next?
And then?
And then what?
And after that?
What about ...?
And what shall I do then?
Anything else?

4. How?

How shall I cut them open?

How shall I remove the seeds?
How shall I stuff them?
How shall I cook them?
How shall I slice them?
How shall I prepare the garlic?

5. **How Long?**

For how long?
How long?
For how many minutes (seconds, hours)?

Giving instructions

Cut each head of cabbage in half.
Boil it in water with lemon juice.
Stuff the peppers with meat.
Put the tomatoes in boiling water (ice-cold water).
Crush the garlic and then grind it.
Scrub the potatoes with a brush.
Do like this. Watch me.
I will show you.
I will demonstrate.

List of important verbs

Wash the asparagus.
Split them down the middle.
Dice the carrots.
Peel the tomatoes.
Boil the corn.
Crush the garlic.
Remove the seeds.
Slice the aubergines (eggplants).
Cut them into small pieces.

Trim off the ends.
Scrub the potatoes.
Make a salad.
Chop the onions fine.
Prepare the garlic.
Grind the garlic.
Stuff the peppers.
Soak the cauliflower.

Proper responses

Yes, please do.
Yes, of course.
Yes. Sure.

That's right.
Right. Go ahead.
Yes. Go right ahead.

No. wait a minute.
No. Please don't.
No. Don't bother.

No, not right now.
No. It's not necessary.
No, not now.

Give It a Try

Task 1

Fill in the blanks with the important verbs we have learnt.

1. _____ the seeds.
2. _____ the peppers.
3. _____ the eggplants.
4. _____ the cauliflower.
5. _____ the asparagus.
6. _____ the ends of the spring onions.
7. _____ them down the middle.
8. _____ the potatoes.
9. _____ the carrots.
10. _____ a salad.
11. _____ the tomatoes.
12. _____ the onions fine.
13. _____ the corn.
14. _____ the garlic.
15. _____ each head of cabbage in half.

Task 2

Make up a conversation between a commis and a chef and then act it out.

Do Extension Activities

Activity 1

Can You Name These Vegetables?

1. Name a long, thin, orange vegetable that grows underground. It starts with a "C."
2. Name a crisp, green vegetable that has long stalks. It starts with a "C."
3. Name a yellow vegetable that grows on a cob and starts with a "C."
4. Name a vegetable that is green on the outside and white on the inside. It starts with a "C."
5. Name a purple vegetable that starts with an "E."
6. Name a green, leafy vegetable that tastes good in salads. It starts with an "L."
7. Name a sharp-tasting vegetable that starts with an "O." It grows underground.
8. Name a tiny, round green vegetable that grows in pods. It starts with a "P."
9. Name a vegetable that is brown on the outside and white on the inside. It grows underground and starts with a "P."
10. Name an orange vegetable that can be made into pie. It starts with a "P."

11. Name a soft, red and round vegetable that starts with a "T." It is not sweet. People also consider it as a fruit.
12. Name a sweet, orange vegetable that starts with a "Y." It grows underground and can be made into pie.

Discuss the following questions with your partner.

1. What is the best and fastest way to peel the tomato?
2. What makes vegetables keep vitamins?
3. How do we choose fresh vegetables?
4. How can we keep the vegetables fresh after we buy them?
5. What kind of vegetables do you like best? Why?

Learning Tips

How to Make a Cheese Omelette (煎蛋)

First, take some eggs. You will need one or two or three.

Next, add some milk and beat the mixture for a few minutes until the mixture is smooth.

After that, add some cheese, some salt and some pepper into the mixture.

Then you melt some butter in a frying pan and pour the egg mixture into the frying pan and cook it for about 3 or 5 minutes. When it is nearly cooked, you fold half of the mixture and cook it for another 3 or 5 minutes. Then take it out and you can eat it. It is quite simple to make an omelet.

Unit 5

Food Material II

Part A BOM

Teaching hours: 2 hours

LEARNING GOALS

To be able to
- know the English names of various fruits
- know some information about fruit
- express likes and dislikes of fruit

VOCABULARY ASSISTANCE

lemon	n.	柠檬	nutritious	adj.	有营养的
chronic	adj.	慢性的,长期的	berry	n.	莓
plum	n.	李子	flavor	n.	味道
kiwi	n.	猕猴桃	mineral	n.	矿物
lichee	n.	荔枝	consume	v.	消耗
pomegranate	n.	石榴	avocado	n.	鳄梨
papaya	n.	木瓜	folate	n.	叶酸
apricot	n.	杏	potassium	n.	钾
tangerine	n.	橘子	ferment	v.	使发酵
turnip	n.	萝卜	substance	n.	物质
blueberry	n.	越莓,蓝莓	instant	adj.	立即的,直接的
star fruit		杨桃	honeydew melon		哈密瓜

Start You Off

Activity 1

Can you name these fruits in English? Try to match the pictures with the words in the box.

lemon	star fruit	banana	water melon	coconut
mango	pineapple	strawberry	cherry	orange
pomegranate	papaya	lichee	apple	peach
honeydew melon				

_____ _____ _____ _____

_____ _____ _____ _____

_____ _____ _____ _____

  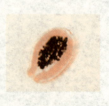 

_____ _____ _____ _____

Activity 2

Can you identify fruits and vegetables? Put the following words into the right box.

cherry	cauliflower	bean	pear	celery
plum	grap	sweet pepper	apricot	tangerine
turnip	pineapple	broccoli	blueberry	carrot

FRUIT	VEGETABLE

Activity 3

Complete the following sentences with missing letters.

1. Put p __ c __ __ __ into the fruit salad.
2. Wash the p __ __ ms.
3. Put cream on the st__ __ __ b __ __ ry.
4. Peel the o __ __ __ g __.
5. Boil the p __ __ rs for five minutes.
6. Slice open the water __ __ __ __ __.
7. Wash the g __ __ p __ s well.
8. Bring me some t __ __ g __ __ i __ __ __.
9. Mash up the __ a __ a __ a __.
10. Serve the clean __ pr __ __ __ t __.

Focus on Language

Fruits and Vegetables

diredions

Questions:

1. Why are fruits and vegetables important to people's health?
2. Have you thought about the colors when you eat fruits and vegetables?
3. What is the good time to eat fruits?

Busy lives can benefit from food that's nutritious, like fresh fruits and vegetables. Fruits and vegetables are a natural source of energy and give the body many nutrients you need to keep going.

Fruits and vegetables come in terrific colors and flavors, but their real beauty lies in what's inside. Fruits and vegetables are great sources of many vitamins, minerals and other natural substances that may help protect you from chronic diseases.

To get a healthy variety, think color. Eating fruits and vegetables of different colors gives your body a wide range of valuable nutrients, like fiber, folate, potassium, and vitamins A and C. Some examples include green spinach, orange sweet potatoes, black beans, yellow corn, purple plums, red watermelon, and white onions. For more variety, try new fruits and vegetables regularly.

Are all the fruits good for health? It depends on your age, the time and amount you consume and your health condition. Apple, grapes, kiwi, berries, pineapple, orange, apricot, plum are in general you can eat any time. Don't eat few fruits just before going to bed. Banana, mangoes, papaya, avocado, are good to have two hours before going to bed. Remember, always eat fruit on an empty stomach. If you eat fruit after dinner the fruit can't be burned properly and will ferment. When eaten before dinner the sugars are burnt immediately, producing instant energy.

⇨ Language Tips

1. The information of fruit

Fruit consists for the largest part of water.
Fruit stimulates our memories.
Fruit makes you feel better.
Fruit is the most natural food.
Fruit is not expensive at all.

Practice 1

How many fruits are mentioned in the passage? What are they?

Practice 2

Write the colors of the following fruits and vegetables. Try to think some more examples.

VEGETABLES AND FRUITS	COLORS
Spinach	
Sweet potatoes	
Beans	
Corn	
Plums	
Watermelon	
Onion	

Practice 3

Discuss the following questions with your partner.

1. Why are fruits and vegetables important to our bodies?
2. What do they contain?
3. What is the best time to eat fruits? Why?
4. What kind of fruits do you like best?
5. What is your habit of eating fruits?

Summarize Key Expressions

1. **Fruits and vegetables are a natural source of energy and give the body many nutrients you need to keep going.**
2. **Fruits and vegetables are great sources of many vitamins, minerals and other natural substances that may help protect you from chronic diseases.**
3. **Eat fruit on an empty stomach.**
4. **Eating fruits and vegetables of different colors gives your body a wide range of valuable nutrients.**
5. **A tomato is the fruit of the tomato plant, but can be used as a vegetable in cooking.**

Give It a Try

Task 1

What do you choose for a fruit salad. And give your reasons.

Task 2

Think about the fruit which has one of the following colors?

| white | green | purple | blue | yellow |
| black | orange | brown | grey | red |

Do Extension Activities

Activity 1

Complete the sentences with the following words.

| exotic | stones | skin | pips |
| varieties | seedless | bitter | bunches |

1. Whatever you do, don't try to eat the _____ of a banana!
2. Plums and peaches have large _____.
3. Grapes and bananas grow in _____.
4. Grapes can be seeded or _____.
5. Grapes have seeds, but lemons and limes have _____.
6. Mangoes, lychees and starfruit are sometimes called tropical or _____ fruit.
7. Golden Delicious, Cox's, and Granny Smith are different _____ of apple.
8. A grapefruit is part of the same family as the orange, but much more _____.

Activity 2

Tick off the odd word in each group.

1. peaches   apples   plums   pumpkin   lychees
2. oranges   apricots   grapes   blackberries   cabbage
3. pineapple   peas   beans   aubergines   carrot
4. celery   eggplant   tangerines   cauliflower   asparagus
5. potatoes   coconut   watermelon   cherries   grapefruit
6. bananas   mangoes   green grapes lemons   onions
7. melon   dates   strawberries pears   peppers
8. papaya   peaches   starfruit   melon   mushroom

Learning Tips

Guidelines for Going to a Pub in England

England has many interesting places that people like to visit. Among them, the pub is often said to be a very special place for visitors to get to know the real life of the English people. The pub is a small "public place," where people can buy beer, soft drinks and even some fast food. What's more, a pub is also a meeting place where people sit and enjoy the beer and talking with their friends. One can easily find a pub at the street corner or in a small village. English people like the pub a lot. After a whole day of busy work, many men spend the whole evening in the pub and go back home at about eleven o'clock when the pub closes.

Part B Fruit Process

Teaching hours: 2 hours

LEARNING GOALS

To be able to
* practise different English terms of processing fruit
* describe how to process fruit in English
* get to know some information about fruits
* be familiar with the ways of handling food

VOCABULARY ASSISTANCE

handle	v.	处理	raw	adj.	生的,未煮熟的
trace	n.	痕迹	poultry	n.	家禽
bacteria	n.	细菌	vomit	v.	呕吐
diarrhoea	n.	腹泻	chopping board		切菜板

Start You Off

Activity 1

How do you process the following fruits?

| banana | pineapple | orange | watermelon |
| kiwi | lemon | grape | papaya |

Activity 2

Write the words of fruit in the proper blanks.

1. Put _____ into the fruit salad.
2. Wash the _____.
3. Soak the _____.
4. Put cream on the _____.

5. Peel the _____.
6. Boil the _____.
7. Slice open the _____.
8. Remove the seeds from the _____.
9. Squeeze the _____.
10. Mash up the _____.

Focus on Language

Handling Food

Dinection

Questions:

1. Do you like cooking?
2. How do you prepare food?
3. What do you need to pay attention to when you prepare meat?
4. What kind of utensils are needed when you prepare food?

Wash and dry hands thoroughly before handling food. When you can, use clean kitchen utensils not fingers for handling foods.

Keep raw and cooked food apart at all times. In particular, keep raw meat, fish, poultry and other raw foods away from cooked foods and ready-to-eat foods (such as salads, bread and sandwiches).

Wash and dry hands, utensils—including chopping boards and knives—and surfaces thoroughly after preparing raw meat, fish, poultry and other raw foods and before contacting with other food. Ideally use separate chopping boards for raw and cooked foods.

Never put cooked food onto a plate which has previously held these raw foods until it has been thoroughly washed.

Do not use the same utensil to stir or serve a cooked meal that was used to prepare the raw ingredients.

Root vegetables such as potatoes, leeks and carrots often have traces of soil on them which can contain harmful bacteria, so wash them thoroughly before use. Don't forget to wash other fruit and vegetables too, especially if they are going to be eaten raw.

Avoid preparing food for yourself or others if you are ill, especially with vomiting and/or diarrhoea.

Language Tips

Wash and dry hands thoroughly before handling food.
Keep raw and cooked food apart at all times.
Wash fruit and vegetables too, especially if they are going to be eaten raw.
Avoid preparing food for yourself or others if you are ill.

Practice 1

What should be done when handling food? Write the verbs in the appropriate box.

hands	
raw and cooked food	
chopping boards	
knives	
plates	
vegetables	
utensils	

Practice 2

Decide whether the following statements are true or false.

1. Wash and dry hands thoroughly after handling food.
2. Use fingers for handling foods instead of kitchen utensils.
3. Keep raw and cooked food apart at all times.
4. Use the same chopping board for raw and cooked foods.
5. We should not wash root vegetables very carefully because they contain nutrients.
6. Avoid preparing food for yourself or others if you are ill.

Practice 3

Complete the following sentences with the information from the passage.

1. Use clean kitchen utensils not _____ for handling foods.
2. Keep _____ and _____ foods apart at all times.
3. Wash _____
   thoroughly after preparing raw meat, fish, poultry and other raw foods.
4. Better use _____ for raw and cooked foods.
5. Root vegetables may contain harmful _____.
6. Avoid preparing food for yourself or others if you are _____.

Summerize Key Expressions

1. Put peaches into the fruit salad.
2. Soak the strawberries.
3. Peel the oranges / bananas / tangerines.
4. Squeeze the lemons / oranges.
5. Remove the seeds from the mangoes / watermelon.
6. Slice open the watermelon / honeydew melon.
7. Mash up the bananas.
8. Refrigerate the melon.
9. Chop up the pineapple.
10. Clean the purple grapes.

Give It a Try

Task 1

Discuss the following questions with a partner.

1. What fruits do you like best?
2. In which season do we have watermelon?
3. Have you had mangoes before?
4. Which do you prefer, apricots or apples?
5. How do you clean the strawberries?

Task 2

Make up a conversation between a commis and a chef, following the examples.

Example 1

Commis: What shall I do?
Chef: Bring me a bunch of purple grapes.
Commis: What do I do with them?
Chef: Wash them well.
Commis: It's not easy to make them clean.
Chef: Soak them in salted water for a while.

Example 2

Commis: What do you want me to do?
Chef: Bring me some fruit.

Commis: What do you need?

Chef: A banana, two apples, a water melon and a pineapple.

Commis: How shall I process them?

Chef: Peel them and dice them.

Commis: What are we going to do with them?

Chef: We are going to make a fruit salad.

Do Extension Activities

Activity 1

Can You Name These Fruits?

1. Name a fruit that starts with an "A." It is white on the inside and can be red, yellow, or green on the outside.
2. Name a long, thin fruit that starts with a "B." It is yellow on the outside and white on the inside.
3. Name a big fruit that starts with a "G." It can be yellow or pink and sometimes squirts you when you eat it.
4. Name a sweet fruit that grows in bunches on vines. It starts with a "G."
5. Name a sour, yellow fruit that starts with an "L."
6. Name a sour, green fruit that starts with an "L."
7. Name a type of big fruit that has a rind. It starts with an "M."
8. Name three sweet fruits that start with a "P" and grow on trees.
9. What do you get when you dry a grape? It starts with a "R."
10. Name a sweet, red fruit that starts with an "S."

Activity 2

How much do you know about food? Here is a questionnaire about food and diet. Answer the questions to find out how much you know about food.

1. Which food gives us a lot of energy the most rapidly?
   A. Cereal.   B. Meat.   C. Fruit.
2. Which of the following helps to build our bodies?
   A. Cereal.   B. Meat.   C. Fruit and vegetable.
3. Which of the following is most fattening?
   A. Brown bread.   B. Boiled potato.   C. Salted peanut.
4. Which of the following do we get a lot of vitamins from?
   A. Cereal.   B. Meat.   C. Fruit and vegetable.

5. People often damage their health by eating too many _____.
   A. breakfast cereal　　　B. fatty food　　　　C. frozen vegetable
6. Which of the following can also be the most dangrous to our health?
   A. Salt.　　　　　　　　B. Tea.　　　　　　　C. Milk.
7. Oranges are good fruit because they contain a lot of _____.
   A. vitamin A　　　　　　B. vitamin B　　　　　C. vitamin C
8. Vitamin C is good for you because it _____.
   A. makes your hair grow
   B. helps to fight colds
   C. helps you to see in the dark
9. Green vegetable like cabbage needs to be cooked _____.
   A. thoroughly　　　　　B. with lots of water　　C. lightly
10. If you live in a cold climate you need a lot of _____.
    A. fat　　　　　　　　B. bread　　　　　　　C. coffee

You can get the right answer for each question from your teacher. The number of your right answers may mean:

0—3　You have little idea about what to eat to keep healthy. You need to find out quickly.

4—7　You have some idea about what to eat to keep healthy, but need to enlarge your mind.

8—10　You have a good knowledge of what you should eat and should not eat. But what do you eat?

Learning Tips

Guidelines for Going to a Dinner Party

When you go to a dinner party, it's a good idea to bring a small gift. Flowers are always nice and welcome, or you may bring some drinks, for example, beer, brandy and something like that. You should arrive on time or not more than five minutes late. Don't get there early. If you are going to be more than fifteen minutes late, you should call them or let them know. Try to be free at the dinner table. If you don't know how to use the fork and knife, don't worry about it. You can watch other people and follow them. When you still have no idea of what to do, ask the person who is next to you. If you like the food, you should say what you think of it. Of course, you should thank the host for the meal after the dinner. Usually a thank-you card is needed after the party.

Unit 6

Food Material III

Part A Beef and Lamb

Teaching hours: 2 hours

LEARNING GOALS

To be able to
* tell the materials and dishes of beef and lamb
* tell the time needed to prepare beef or lamb dish
* tell the ingredients for making beef or lamb dish
* tell the process of making beef or lamb dish

VOCABULARY ASSISTANCE

fillet	n.	肉片,鱼片	cutlet	n.	肉排,肉片
chop	n.	一块(肉、排骨)	chuck	n.	牛颈部至肩部的肉
brisket	n.	胸肉	sirloin	n.	牛腰肉
shank	n.	(牛羊等的)腿	plate	n.	侧胸腹肉
tenderloin	n.	腰部嫩肉	flank	n.	牛肋腹肉
round	n.	牛腿肉	slice	v.& n.	切片,薄片
grill	v.	烤	sauté	v.& adj.	煎(的)
braise	v.	焖	brochette	n.	烤肉
loin	n.	腰肉	rump	n.	后腿部的牛排
broccoli	n.	花椰菜,花茎甘蓝	scallion	n.	大葱
cubed	adj.	(正方)块状的	pint	n.	(量词)品脱
marinate	v.	浸泡	slant	adj.	斜的
segment	n.	部分,一小块	cornmeal	n.	(粗磨)玉米粉
simmer	v.	慢慢地煮	blade	n.	肩胛骨
chunk	n.	(厚)块	gradient	n.	梯度
prime rib		主肋骨,大肋骨	3 cloves of garlic		三瓣蒜
per your taste		按照您的口味			

Unit 6

Start You Off

Activity 1

Look at the materials and dishes of beef and lamb below and do the question and answer practice in pairs.

A: What is this?
B: It's a _____.

beef fillet   beef T-bone   beef tongue

beef rib   lamb leg   lamb cutlet

lamb loin chops   lamb shoulder   sautéed mutton with scallion

lamb curry   pepper steak   lamb with beans

Now look at the ox below and remember the name of the meat at each part.

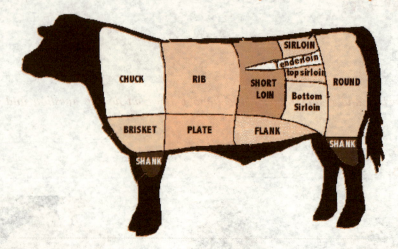

Activity 2

The following pictures show people who work in the kitchen. Look at the pictures below, and try to find out what they are doing. Match the phrases in the box with the corresponding pictures.

| braise a beef | stew a veal | season a lamb rack | grill a steak |
| carve a lamb | slice a beef | wrap a beef | sauté mutton |

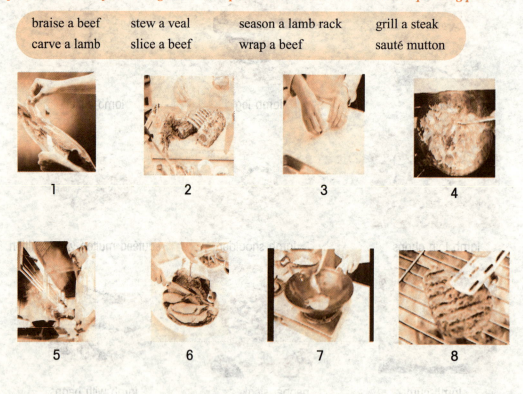

Focus on Language

Listen to the following passage and read it. Then answer the questions.

The tenderness of cooked steak is influenced by how much it is done. Depending on the time for which the steak is cooked, it may be raw, very rare, rare, medium rare, medium, medium well-done and well-done. Rare steaks are exposed to the flame for a very short time. They still maintain their rawness and are very pink in color. Rarely done steaks maintain their original beefy flavors, but they are not very healthy as they still contain microorganisms. As the cooking time increases, the pinkness of steak gets converted to brownness and its juiciness also reduces. Medium steaks are pink in the center, grayish brown at the surroundings. Well-done steaks are brown throughout and also tough to chew.

Questions:

1. What influences the tenderness of cooked steak?
2. How can you tell the steaks are rare, medium or well-done?
3. Do you prefer the steaks rare, medium or well-done? Why?

Language Tips

1. The dish ordered and the time to make it

◆ How long does it take to make a well-done steak?
◇ It takes about 4 minutes.
   You have to grill it for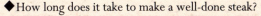
◆ What did the customer order?
◇ He ordered (wanted) a tenderloin steak and a veal cutlets.
◆ What did he want to go with (accompany) the steak?
◇ With a baked potato.
◆ Did he want the steak to be well-done, medium or rare?
◇ He wanted it to be 90 percent well-done.

Practice 1

Look at the chart below, and practice in pairs to ask and answer the time needed to make the dishes along the left of the chart.

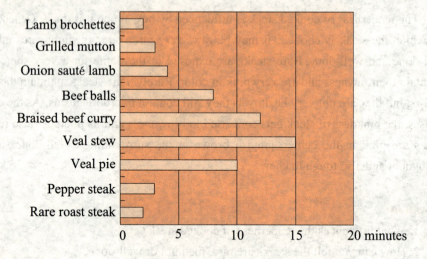

Practice 2

Work in groups and give the names of the beef or lamb dishes you have made. Then tell the time to make these dishes.

Practice 3

Role-play asking what the customer wants for main dish and companion. Take turns and do like this:

    W=Waiter   C=Cook
    C: What did the customers order?
    W: They wanted a <u>prime rib steak and a veal stew</u>.
    C: What did they want to accompany the steak?
    W: With a <u>baked potato</u>.
    C: Did they want the steak well-done, medium or rare?
    W: How long does it take to grill a steak well-done?
    C: It takes about 4 minutes.
    W: Then make it well-done. They can afford to wait.

Practice the conversation in pairs and substitute the underlined words with the following dishes and companions.

Dish 1	Dish 2	Companion
rump steak	rack of veal	a baked broccoli
sirloin steak	shoulder of veal	some fried rice
T-bone steak	roast loin of veal	3 loafs of bread
pepper steak	veal pie	2 grilled tomatoes

2. The ingredients needed to make beef or lamb dish

◆ What do you need to prepare for a sautéed mutton with scallion?
What are the ingredients?
We need 200 grams of lamb slices, 2 scallions, a teaspoon of minced ginger and garlic, and some seasonings.

Practice 1

Look at the recipe below for a western-style lamb curry, and work in pairs telling what are exactly needed. For abbreviations, look at the following table for reference.

4 lb. cubed lamb
3 cloves garlic, minced
1 $\frac{1}{2}$ tsp. curry powder
2 cans of mushroom soup
1 tsp. salt

1 c. chopped onion
1/2 c. milk
4 tbsp. butter
2 c. sour cream

tbsp.	stands for	tablespoon	oz.	stands for	ounce
tsp.	stands for	teaspoon	pt.	stands for	pint
c.	stands for	cup	lb.	stands for	pound

A: What do you need to make lamb curry?
B: We need 4 pounds of cubed lamb, 1 cup of chopped onion, 3 cloves of minced garlic, half a cup of milk, one and a half teaspoons of curry powder, 4 tablespoons of butter, 2 cans of mushroom soup, 2 cups of sour cream and 1 teaspoon of salt.

Now work in pairs using the following recipe.

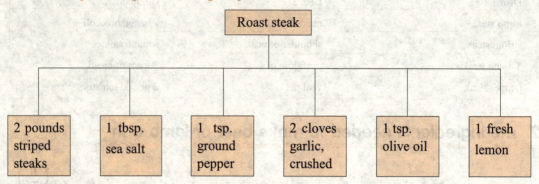

Practice 2

Listen to the conversation. Write down the name of the dish they made and then make a tick to the ingredients mentioned.

Name of the dish: _____
- ☐ 200 grams of lamb slice
- ☐ 1 tsp. ginger, minced
- ☐ 2 tbsp. butter
- ☐ 1 tbsp. sauce
- ☐ some salt and sugar
- ☐ 2 scallions
- ☐ 1 tsp. vinegar
- ☐ 1 tsp. ground garlic

3. How to make a dish

◆ Cook the meat over medium heat　　for 10 minutes.
　　　　　　　　　　　　　　　　until tender.

◆ Choose the seasoning per your taste.

◆ When　　shall I put the mutton slice into the oil?
　At what time

◇ Put in the mutton when the oil is boiling in the pan.

◆ Put in the scallion segments when the meat is half done.

Unit 6

Practice 1

Listen to the conversation. Then try to find the answers to the following questions.

1. Did the student cook the beef over low heat?
2. What did the student add to the beef?
3. Did the student cook the beef for another five to fifteen minutes?

Practice 2

Fill in the blanks with the words that you will hear on the tape.

A senior chef is presenting how to make a western-style lamb curry. The following is what he says:

For preparation, you need to cut the lamb into cubes and marinate it in wine for _____. To start, you need to cook onion and garlic in butter. Stir in curry powder. Then drain lamb from wine and add it to onion mixture, cook covered over _____ for 10 minutes, stirring frequently. Add salt, soup, milk and wine. Then cook in _____ for 2 hours. Stir in sour cream and heat. Choose the _____ per your taste. _____.

Practice 3

Role-play the sequence in making sautéed mutton with scallion. Take turns being the student and the chef by following the model below.

S=Student   C=Chef

S: The meat has been cut to slices, and the scallion has been cut to slant segments. What shall we do next?

C: Turn the stove to the maximum, and pour 3 tablespoons of olive oil into the pan.

S: When shall I put in the mutton?

C: When the oil is boiling, put in half of the ginger and garlic; and when the ginger smells, put in the mutton slices.

S: Then shall I stir-fry the mutton?

C: Yes. When the meat is half done, put in the scallion segments, and keep stir-frying.

S: For how long?

C: Till the scallion is soft, and then shut the stove. Dress it with the other half of garlic and ginger.

S: And how about the seasoning?

C: Season with a tablespoon of sauce and a teaspoon of vinegar during the cooking. Then add salt or sugar per your taste.

Summarize Key Expressions

1. **Asking about the dish that the customer wants**

   a. What did the customer order?

   b. What did he want to accompany the main dish?

   c. How did he want the dish to be cooked?

   d. Did he want it well-done, medium or rare?

2. **Giving the time needed to prepare a dish or for a step in making a dish**

   a. It totally takes about 10 minutes to make a veal pie.

   b. You have to grill the steak for 4 minutes to make it well-done.

   c. You need 4 minutes to grill the steak well-done.

   d. Remember to marinate the lamb in the wine for 8 hours.

   e. Stir-fry the mutton slices for 1 minute.

   f. Cook the meat over medium heat for 10 minutes.

3. **Asking for the ingredients of a dish**

   a. What do you need to prepare for a lamb curry?

   b. What ingredients are needed to make a lamb curry?

   c. What is the recipe for a lamb curry?

   d. What are necessary for making a lamb curry?

4. **The actions during the making of the dish**

   a. Cut the beef into cubes.

   b. Stir in curry powder.

   c. Braise (stew, boil) the veal for 10 minutes.

   d. Roast (grill, bake, barbecue) the steak till well-done.

   e. Season with a tablespoon of sauce and a teaspoon of vinegar.

   f. Turn the steak once and rearrange during the grilling.

5. **Sequence in making a dish**

   a. Put in the mutton slices when the oil is boiling in the pan.

   b. Keep stewing the veal till the steam comes out.

   c. Shut the stove once the scallions are soft.

   d. The moment the coal is red hot, place the steaks on the grill.

Give It a Try

Task 1

The chef is giving instruction on how to make a dish. Listen and write down the information you will hear.

Name of the dish:	
What are needed:	
Work before cooking:	
When to stop sautéing meat:	
How to treat pepper:	
Time for simmering:	
What to serve over:	

Task 2

The following is an instruction on cooking an easy beef soup. First rearrange the following steps in correct order. Then make a presentation to the class on how to cook it.

1. Season to taste with salt and pepper.
2. Add carrots, potatoes, onion and cornmeal; simmer until vegetables are tender.
3. In a large saucepan cook the beef in the water until tender.
4. Add more water if desired.

Do Extension Activities

Activity 1

Work in pairs to make a conversation. One acts as a student, and the other acts as a cook. The student is going to make an easy western lamb dish.

Conversational tips for the student:
1. I'm going to make...

2. How long does it take ...?
3. What are the ingredients for ...?
4. How to make...?
5. How many people can it serve?

Conversational tips for the cook:
1. If you want the lamb well-done, you need to heat it 1 hour.
2. Here are the ingredients: 3 tbsp. butter; 4 lamb shoulders or blades or arm chops, about 1 inch thick; 1 can pineapple; 1 green pepper, chopped; 1 tbsp. soy sauce.
3. Here is the process:

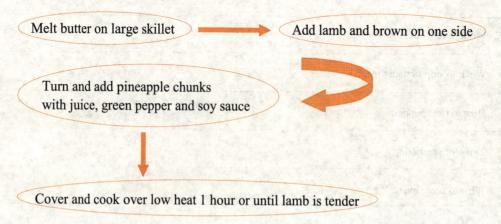

4. It serves only 1 person.

Activity 2

Go to the kitchen and try to find a microwave oven and the following ingredients: 8 lamb chops; 2 tbsp. butter; 1 tbsp. flour; 1/2 tsp. salt; 1/4 tsp. garlic powder; 1/8 tsp. pepper; 8 oz. mushrooms, sliced. We are going to make a mushroom lamb chops. Role-play one asking the sequence for making it and one answering according to the following sequence.

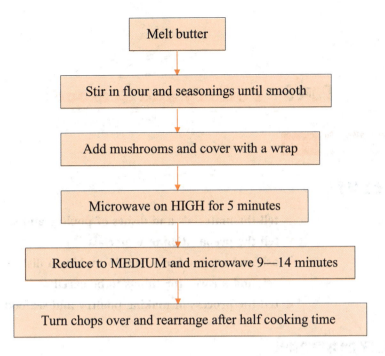

Learning Tips

Tips to Grill a Perfect Steak

1. Light the coals at least one hour before you expect to grill.
2. Season meat one hour before cooking with salt and freshly ground pepper.
3. Allow the meat to come to room temperature before cooking.
4. Before you start cooking, make sure you have a gradient of heat.
5. Rub your meat with a little oil before you grill.
6. Start grilling the food that will take the longest first.
7. Start cooking your meat on high heat (that is, over the highest coals).
8. Allow the meat to rest for at least 10 minutes after you pull it off the grill.

Part B Poultry and Seafood

Teaching hours: 2 hours

LEARNING GOALS

To be able to
* tell the materials and dishes of poultry and seafood
* tell the preparation of materials
* ask and answer for advice in making a dish
* ask and answer for things to be cared
* tell the process of making poultry and seafood dish

VOCABULARY ASSISTANCE

mallard	n.	野鸭	trout	n.	鳟鱼
tuna	n.	金枪鱼	salmon	n.	三文鱼
mussel	n.	贻贝	oyster	n.	牡蛎
scallop	n.	扇贝	rind	n.	外皮
celery	n.	芹菜	nip	v.	掐
pierce	v.	刺穿	gravy	n.	肉汤
saturated	adj.	浸透的;充满的	moisture	n.	水分
crunchy	adj.	脆的	texture	n.	质地
parsley	n.	欧芹	giblet	n.	内脏
stuffing	n.	填充物	compress	v.	挤压
sew	v.	缝	drumstick	n.	家禽腿下部
egg wash		蛋汁			

Start You Off

Activity 1

Look at the materials of poultry and seafood below and do the question and answer practice in pairs.

Unit 6

A: Is this _____?
B: Yes, it is. (No, it isn't.)

chicken leg   duck (mallard)   turkey

goose   crab   lobster

oyster   shrimp   tuna

trout   mussel   salmon

Activity 2

Suppose you are cooking the following dish, and role-play as the following.

A: What are you cooking?
B: I am cooking _____. (Look at the pictures below.)

fried shrimp

roast duck

baked fish

curry mussel

fried chicken

baked lobster

stuffed turkey

oyster soup

scallop salad

grilled tuna

Focus on Language

Listen to the passage about the storing of seafood and fill in the blanks.

    Store your seafood in the refrigerator if you intend to use it within two days after purchase. In case you will not use your seafood within two days after purchase, wrap it in moisture-proof paper or plastic wrap, place it in a heavy_____, or put it in an airtight, rigid container, and store it in the_____. Keep the temperature of the refrigerator between_____, and of your freezer at_____ as close to _____ as possible.

Unit 6

1. Tips on the preparation of materials

◆ How to store the seafood for two days?
◇ Store it in a refrigerator or a rigid container.
◆ What shall we do with the shrimps before frying them?
   Could you advise me on how to treat
◇ We should peel them, and de-head and de-vein.
◆ Do you have anything to remind me of?
◇ Make sure to drain the shrimps off the egg wash.

Practice 1

Look at the recipes below and work in pairs telling what ingredients are needed.

Lemon-roasted duck	Shrimp curry	Oyster soup
4 mallards	1 pint of oysters	3 pints of oysters
salt	3 tablespoons of butter	1 pint of milk
pepper	3 tablespoons of flour	2 eggs
1 stick of butter	milk	3 tablespoons of butter
juice and rind of 2 lemons	1/2 teaspoon of curry powder	1 slice of ham
	salt	1 stalk of celery

Do the question and answer practice in pairs like this:

A: Do you need butter to make a shrimp curry?
B: Yes, we need 3 tablespoons of butter.

Practice 2

For preparations of poultry and seafood, one needs to use certain verbs. Choose from column B the correct translation of the verbs in column A.

A	B
1. pluck	a. 剔除鱼刺
2. cube	b. 去头
3. remove	c. 去壳
4. scale	d. 去泥肠
5. slice	e. 去鱼鳞
6. split	f. 拔毛

7. de-vein   g. 去皮
8. stuff   h. 去掉
9. shell   i. 填充
10. peel   j. 切成片状
11. de-head   k. 切成方块
12. bone (the fish)   l. 切开

Practice 3

Role-play acting as chef and student asking for advice like the following.

S=Student   C=Chef

C: Do you have a problem cooking fried shrimps?
S: Yes. Could you advise me on how to treat the shrimps before frying them?
C: Peel the body, nip off the head and pull out the vein.
S: What's the best way to clean the shrimps?
C: Wash them with cold water.
S: Do you have anything to remind me of before cooking?
C: You should dip the shrimps into a bowl of egg wash. Then make sure to drain them off the egg before cooking.

2. Tips on the process of making a dish

◆ Where shall we start with?
◇ First you should wash and dry the bird.
◆ What shall we do next?
◇ Next brown the duck in the melted butter.
◆ What is the last step?
◇ Finally remove meat from bones.
◆ When should I stop roasting?
◇ Till the duck is pierced with a fork.
◆ What is the dish served with?
◇ It is served with rice. It serves 3 guests.

Practice 1

Listen to the recording and complete the following conversation. Then do the conversation in pairs.

S=Student   C=Chef

S: We are going to make a _____. Where shall we start with?

C: Wash and dry the bird. Rub with flour and sprinkle all over with _____.

S: _____?

C: Melt the butter in a pan and brown the duck _____.

S: _____?

C: Yes, roast the duck in an oven at 350 degrees for 45 minutes to 1 hour, uncovered, _____.

S: Which side should be up during the roasting?

C: The breast side of the duck.

S: _____?

C: Finally, _____ and pour gravy in pan over meat.

Practice 2

Role-play acting as cook and student asking for advice.

S=Student   C=Cook

S: Do I have to pretreat the fish before baking it?

C: Yes, you should cut the fish into fillets.

S: How to make the meat tender?

C: The key is to put some salt onto the fillet.

S: How long and at what temperature shall I bake it?

C: Bake covered for 45 minutes at 350 degrees and uncovered for 15 minutes at 350 degrees.

S: What is it served with?

C: The baked fish is served well with rice.

Summarize Key Expressions

1. **Asking for help or suggestion**
    a. Could you give me any advice?
    b. Could you advise me on how to treat the shrimps before frying them?
    c. How to make the meat tender?
    d. Do you have anything to remind me of?
    e. What should I pay attention to?

2. Asking about the process of making a dish
   a. Where shall we start with?
   b. What shall we do next?
   c. What is the last step?
   d. When should I stop cooking?

3. Telling about the preparations of poultry and seafood
   a. Wash and dry the bird before cooking.
   b. Pluck a chicken.
   c. Peel the body, nip off the head and pull out the vein.
   d. Remove giblets and neck.
   e. Store the seafood in the refrigerator.

4. Telling the process of making poultry and seafood dish
   a. First we should cut the fish into fillets.
   b. Rub the flour and sprinkle all over with salt and pepper.
   c. Roast the duck till it is pierced with a fork.
   d. Finally remove meat from bones.

5. Reminding of what should be cared
   a. Make sure to drain the shrimps off the egg wash before cooking.
   b. Remember to do so.
   c. See to it that the duck is well covered during the roasting.
   d. The key is to put some salt onto the fillet.

6. Talking about the temperature and the time needed
   a. Roast the duck at 350 degrees for 45 minutes to 1 hour.
   b. Cook the fish at 400 degrees for twenty to twenty-five minutes.
   c. Cook the chicken over medium heat for twenty minutes.
   d. Roast the turkey at 325 degrees for 4 hours.
   e. Cook the chicken over low heat until light brown.

Give It a Try

The teacher is giving instruction on how to make a dish. Listen and write down the information you have heard.

Unit 6

Name of the dish:	
What are needed:	
How to treat chicken:	
What should be cared about:	
How to see it is done:	
Time for frying:	
What to serve with:	

Task 2

The following is an instruction on how to make curried mussels. Read it carefully and make a presentation to the class on how to make the dish and describe it, using words denoting sequences like "first, then, next, finally, etc."

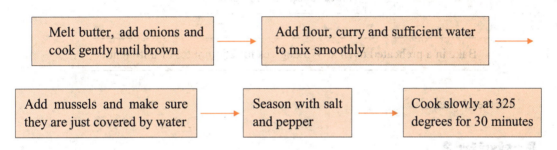

Do Extension Activities

Activity 1

Role-play according to the following situation. Do it in pairs. Student A will be the student and student B will be the chef.

Student:
  You want to bake lobster tails.
  You want to know what ingredients are needed.
  You want to know how to pretreat the lobster before cooking.
  You want to know how to make the dish.
  You want to know how many people it can serve.

Chef:
  Here are the ingredients: 3 lobster tails, 2 tsp. parsley, 1 tsp. salt,
  3 tbsp. olive oil, juice of 1 lemon, 1 c. water

109

The process:

```
Split lobster tails in half lengthwise
            ↓
Remove sharp edges
            ↓
Sprinkle each with parsley and salt
            ↓
Pour olive oil and lemon juice on each tail
            ↓
Pour water on the bottom of a baking pan
            ↓
Place lobster tails in pan
            ↓
Bake in a preheated oven at 375 degrees for 25 minutes or until tender
```

It serves 3 guests.

Activity 2

Turkey is a traditional food for holidays. Here is a way to make stuffed turkey. Translate it into Chinese. Role-play asking and answering about what should be cared during the making of the dish. Try to cook a turkey for your family on a holiday.

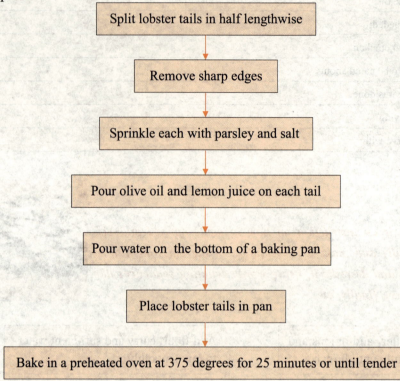

1. Wash turkey under cold running water; remove giblets, neck, etc. from inside and save for making giblet gravy.
2. To make stuffing, sauté mushroom, onion and celery in the butter until tender. Mix them with rice.
3. Spoon stuffing mixture into neck and body holes lightly; do not compress; sew opening closed with string; tie legs together.
4. Place turkey's breast side up on a rack in a deep pan; roast, uncovered, at 325°F for 4 hours or until drumstick offers little resistance when moved.
5. Remember that 20 pounds of turkey can serve 5 people.

Unit 7

Making a Meal

Part A   Making an Appetizer

Teaching hours: 2 hours

LEARNING GOALS

To be able to
* tell what an appetizer is
* talk about the types of appetizers
* discuss the ingredients

VOCABULARY ASSISTANCE

fish	n.	鱼	mushroom	n.	蘑菇
watermelon	n.	西瓜	bacon	n.	培根
pineapple	n.	菠萝	peanut	n.	花生
shellfish	n.	贝	butter	n.	黄油
fork	n.	叉子	chopstick	n.	筷子
cocktail	n.	鸡尾酒	appetizer	n.	开胃菜
hors-d'oeuvre	n.	餐前小吃	canapé	n.	鸡尾小吃
relish	n.	酸果,泡菜	strawberry	n.	草莓
apple	n.	苹果	tomato	n.	番茄
prawn	n.	对虾	beef	n.	牛肉
chicken	n.	鸡	olive oil		橄榄油
tea cup		茶杯	sea cucumber		海参
coffee pot		咖啡壶	measuring cup		量杯
tin opener		开罐器	chicken liver pate		鸡肝酱
mixed BBQ skewer		什锦烧烤串	Kewpie mayonnaise		千岛酱
North Pole calm		北极贝	lemon juice		柠檬汁
BBQ Skewer		烧烤串			
smoked salmon canapés		熏三文鱼鸡尾小吃			

Start You Off

Activity 1

Look at the pictures below, tell their English names and do question and answer practice in pairs as the example given.

Example:

    A: What is this?
    B: It's an onion.
    A: And what is that?
    B: That is salt.

Unit 7

Activity 2

Look at the pictures, tell their English names and make conversations by using the patterns below.

A: What is... ?
B: ... is something you... with.
A: How about... ?
B: It is what you can use to...

Focus on Language

Listen to the tape and answer the following questions.

1. What is appetizer?
2. How is it called in French?
3. What can it also apply to?

Language Tips

1. Talking about the types of appetizers

◆ Is appetizer a main course?
◇ No, it is not. It is something you start your meal with.
◆ How many types of appetizers are there in western food?
◇ There are mainly 5 types.
◆ What are they?
◇ They are cocktail, appetizer salad, hors-d'oeuvre, canapes and relishes.
◆ I see.

Practice 1

Look at the cookery book, find out the appetizers of each type and speak out their English names.

Practice 2

Role-play: Student A plays the role of a waiter; student B plays the role of a diner. Follow the example below and practice making a similar conversation about appetizer.

Example: A: What do you want to start your meal with, madam?
           B: A chicken liver pate, please.
           A: What kind of appetizer do you prefer, sir?
           B: A smoked salmon canapes will do, I think.

Practice 3

Work with your partner, translate the following into Chinese and find out which one is an appetizer in each group.

Unit 7

1	Potato & Bacon Salad	Sautéed Beef Fillet with Black Pepper	Sautéed Perch in Spicy Soybean Paste
2	Stewed Chicken with Curry	Relishes	Sautéed Crab in Hot and Spicy Sauce
3	Barbecued Spare Rib	Braised Sea Cucumber in Soy Sauce	Chicken Galantine
4	Steamed River Crab	Pate de Foie Gras	Pan-fried Sole
5	Hare Pie	Braised Chicken with Red Wine	Spaghetti with Seafood

2. Discussing the ingredients

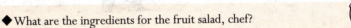

◆ What are the ingredients for the fruit salad, chef?
◇ They are strawberry, apple, egg and Kewpie mayonnaise.
◆ What do we need for the vegetable salad?
◇ We need tomato, cucumber, bacon, olive oil, salt and pepper.
◆ How about / What about seafood salad?
◇ For seafood salad, you have to prepare salmon, North Pole calm, scallop, pearl oyster, lemon juice, olive oil, salt and pepper.

Practice 1

Pair work: Look at the cookery book, follow the sample conversation given above and practice talking about the ingredients needed for a dish, a soup, a barbecue, a dessert etc. by using the following patterns.

What are the ingredients for...?
What do we need for...?
How about/ What about...?

Practice 2

Look at the pictures below and practice talking about what ingredients are needed for each appetizer.

fruit salad

seafood salad

baked oyster

goose liver pie

Practice 3

Role-play: Student A plays the role of a waiter; student B plays the role of a diner. Follow the example and make a similar conversation about ordering food and about the ingredients.

Example:

A: Can I take your order, sir?

B: Sure. I'll have a French Onion Soup, two pieces of bread and a Mixed BBQ Skewer. By the way, what are the ingredients for the BBQ Skewer?

A: They are scallop, prawn, beef, chicken, green-red pepper, onion, olive oil, BBQ sauce, salt and pepper.

B: Sounds delicious. I'll have one of that.

A: Just a minute, sir.

Summarize Key Expressions

1. Asking about the types of appetizers

   a. How many types of appetizer are there, chef?
      There are altogether 5 types of appetizer.

   b. What are the types of starters?

The types of starters are cocktail, appetizer salad, hors-d'oeuvre, canapés and relishes.
   c. What sort of appetizer does this restaurant offer?
      This restaurant offers appetizer salad and relishes.

2. **Discussing the ingredients**
   a. What are the ingredients of the seafood salad, chef?
      For seafood salad, we'll have salmon, North Pole calm, scallop, pearl oyster, lemon juice, olive oil, salt and pepper.
   b. What ingredients should I prepare for the appetizer, chef?
      You have to prepare veal, mushroom, butter, salt and pepper.
   c. What ingredients do we need for the starter, chef?
      We need tomato, cucumber, bacon, olive oil, salt and pepper.

Give It a Try

Task 1

Work in groups talking about the types of Chinese dishes by using the following sentences.

   A: Do you like Chinese dishes?
   B: Of course.
   A: How many types of ... ?
   B: Generally speaking, there are ...types.
   A: What are they?
   B: They are ...
   A: I see.

Task 2

Role-play: Student A plays the role of a husband; student B plays the role of a wife. List the appetizers for a party and discuss the ingredients to be prepared.

Do Extension Activities

Activity 1

Look at the cookery book, find out the typical appetizer of each type (cocktail, appetizer salads, hors-d'oeuvre, canapés and relishes), speak out the ingredients and learn them by heart.

Activity 2

Group work: Divide the class into several groups and ask the students to work out a menu of appetizers with their groupmates.

Activity 3

Listen to the tape and answer the following questions.

1. What is canape?
2. Why are canapes often either salty or spicy?
3. What may a canape be also referred to?

Activity 4

Listen to the tape and put the following ingredients of different appetizers into the right place.

Fruit Cocktail 水果头盘

_____, _____, _____, _____, strawberry, lemon juice

Smoked Salmon Canapés 熏三文鱼鸡尾小吃

toast, smoked salmon, _____, _____, cheese powder, lemon juice, salt

Pate de Foie Gras 鹅肝酱

foie gras, goose oil, fresh cream, sherry, _____, bay leaf, thyme, nutmeg, _____, _____, _____.

Learning Tips

Salad

Salad is a mixture of cold foods, usually including vegetables or fruits, often with a dressing and sometimes with the addition of meat, fish, pasta, cheese, or whole grains. Salad is often served as an appetizer before a larger meal. The word "salad" comes from the French *salade* of the same meaning, which in turn is from the Latin *salata*.

Unit 7

Part B   Making Soup

Teaching hours: 2 hours

LEARNING GOALS

To be able to
* classify soup
* tell how to prepare the ingredients
* tell the process of preparing the ingredients

VOCABULARY ASSISTANCE

wine	n.	葡萄酒	sprite	n.	烈性酒
peel	v.	削皮	shred	v.	切（丝）
soft drink		软饮料	clear soup ("consommé" in French)		清汤
puree soup		茸汤	cream soup		奶油汤
thick soup (broth)		浓汤	vegetable soup		蔬菜汤
seafood soup		海鲜汤	iced soup		冷汤
consommé German		德式清汤	green pea puree soup		青豆茸汤
cream asparagus soup		芦笋奶油汤	French onion soup		法式洋葱汤
lobster bisque		龙虾浓汤	cold fruit soup		水果冷汤

Start You Off

Listen and complete the following conversation.

A: Are you ready to _____ now?
B: I want to have _____ to _____ first.
A: Do you want _____ drink, _____, _____ or _____?
B: I want to have _____. Do you have _____ and _____ soup?
A: _____.
B: Ok. I'll have the soup and some tea, _____ tea, please.
A: One _____, sir.

119

Focus on Language

Listen to the tape and fill in the blanks.

Soup is a _____ that is made by combining _____ such as _____ or _____ in stock or hot/_____ water, until the _____ is extracted, forming a _____.

Language Tips

1. Discussing soup

◆ Can you tell me how to classify western soup, chef?
◇ Sure. There are mainly 7 types.
◆ What are they?
◇ They are clear soup ("consommé" in French), puree soup, cream soup, thick soup (broth), vegetable soup, seafood soup and iced soup.
◆ Can you give an example of each of these 7 types of soup?
◇ Of course. For instance, "consommé" German, green pea puree soup, cream asparagus soup, French onion soup, lobster bisque and cold fruit soup.
◆ Thank you for telling me, chef.

Practice 1

The following are some western soups. Translate them into Chinese, identify the type of soup each of them belongs to and make a conversation talking about western soup.

carrots puree soup
cream of mushroom soup
French onion soup
chicken broth
consommé julienne
lobster bisque
cold fruit soup

Practice 2

The following are some Chinese soups. Translate them into Chinese and make conversations about Chinese soup by using the words given in the box.

1. Duck in Aweto Soup

2. Tomato and Egg Soup
3. Spare Rib and Turnip Soup
4. Fish Fillet Soup
5. Fish Head and Fresh Mushroom Soup
6. Sea Cucumber Soup, Shandong Style
7. Chinese Cabbage and Tofu Soup
8. Borscht Soup
9. Shredded Pork and Preserved Vegetable Soup
10. Bamboo Fungus and White Fungus Soup

> order, type, recommend, for instance, try, pleasant to mouth, ingredients, tasty, soup, Chinese, delicious, vegetable

2. Preparing the ingredients

◆ What ingredients should I prepare for the soup, chef?
◇ You have to prepare potato, onion, bacon, eggs etc.
◆ What shall I do with them?
◇ Peel the potato and onion; chop them into slices.
◆ How about bacon and eggs?
◇ Shred the bacon and whisk the eggs finely.
◆ Okay.

Practice 1

Pair-work: Look at the cookery book, find out the kind of soup you are familiar with, make a conversation talking about preparing the ingredients for that soup by imitating the sample conversation given above.

Practice 2

Listen to the tape about "Chilled Tomato and Red Sweet Pepper Soup," "Oyster Soup" and put all the Ingredients and the Steps of preparing the ingredients given below into the right place in the chart.

Ingredients

red sweet pepper   oyster   butter   celery

| flour | lemon | carrot | tomato |
| white wine | onion | salt | pepper |

Steps of preparing the ingredients
- peel the tomato, onion and carrot
- chop tomato, onion, carrot and celery into small dices
- wash the red sweet pepper and remove the seeds
- chop the tomato into slices
- mix the butter in flour, add oyster, white wine, salt and pepper
- melt the butter in a pan
- chop the celery and onion into dices
- peel the lemon and blender it into juice
- clean the oyster
- peel the onion

Chilled Tomato and Red Sweet Pepper Soup	
Ingredients	Steps of preparing the ingredients

Oyster Soup	
Ingredients	Steps of preparing the ingredients

Practice 3

Pair-work: Think of a dish you know how to cook, speak out the ingredients for that dish and then make a conversation talking about how to prepare the ingredients.

Unit 7

3. Processing the preparation of the ingredients

◆ Shall I peel the potatoes first?
◇ Yes, with the peeler.
◆ And then?
◇ Chop the potatoes into slices.
◆ What shall I do next?
◇ Rinse them and then put them into the plate.

Practice 1

Look at the pictures below, speak out the steps of preparing the apple, mashed potatoes, fish and minced garlic. And then make a conversation talking about the process of preparing the ingredients for a soup or a dish as the sample conversation given above.

| apple | first step | second step | third step | fourth step |

| mashed potatoes | first step | second step | third step | fourth step |

| fish | first step | second step | third step | fourth step |

| minced garlic | first step | second step | third step | fourth step |

Practice 2

Translate the following conversation into Chinese.

(A: Commis   B: Chef)

A: How shall I deal with the tomatoes?
B: Wash the tomatoes first.
A: And then?
B: Cut out the centers.
A: What shall I do next?
B: Put the tomatoes in the boiling water for 15 seconds.
A: After that?
B: Put them in the cold water immediately.
A: Why?
B: To peel them easily.
A: I see. What will we use the tomatoes for?
B: Tomato soup.

Summarize Key Expressions

1. Classifying soup

a. Can you tell me how to classify western soup, chef?
   Sure/ Of course/ Certainly/No problem.
b. How many types of western soup are there altogether?
   There are mainly 7 types.
c. What are the 7 types?
   They are clear soup, puree soup, cream soup, thick soup, vegetable soup, seafood soup and iced soup.

2. Preparing the ingredients

a. What ingredients should I prepare for the soup, chef?
   You have to prepare potato, onion, bacon, eggs etc.
b. What shall I do with all these ingredients?
   Peel the potato and onion and chop them into slices.
c. How to deal with the ingredients, chef?
   Shred the bacon and whisk the eggs finely.
d. Shall I peel the onions? Grind the garlic?
   Yes/ No, you don't have to.

3. **Discussing the sequence of preparing the ingredients**

    a. What shall I do first, chef?

       Wash the cucumber first and then peel it.

    b. And then?

       Peel the potatoes.

    c. What shall I do next?

       Next, you have to chop them into pieces.

    d. After that?

       After that, you have to rinse them well.

    e. Is that all?

       Of course not.

    f. What else should I do/ prepare?

       Puree the chicken fillets in the blender.

Give It a Try

Task 1

Listen to the conversation and write out the missing words.

A: For how many _____ do I have to _____ the cauliflower?
B: At _____ three times.
A: How about _____?
B: You don't _____ to.

Task 2

Match the words in column A with the words in column B.

A	B
whisk	potato
peel	garlic
scale	egg
crush	fish

Task 3

Pair-work: Make conversations about preparing the ingredients for soup by using the following patterns.

A: How shall I ... ?
B: First of all ...
A: And then?
B: ...
A: What shall I do next?
B: ...
A: After that?
B: ...
A: What shall I do at last?
B: ...

Do Extension Activities

Activity 1

Translate the following sentences into English.

1. 西餐中的汤类菜肴大致可以分为7类。
2. 西餐清汤的原料不同，因此清汤可分为牛清汤、鸡清汤、鱼清汤。
3. 西餐茸汤根据制作方法和用料的不同，主要分为两种类型。

Activity 2

Translate the following sentences into Chinese.

1. How shall I do with the lettuce, chef?
   Soak the lettuce in salted water.
2. Shall I make the soup with potatoes?
   No. It's not necessary.
3. Do we use frozen peas or tinned today?
   Neither. We'll have fresh peas today.

Activity 3

There are several steps in preparing the green pepper for a dish. Listen to the tape and write out the steps.

The first step: _____
The second step: _____
The third step: _____

The fourth step: _____
The last step: _____

Activity 4

Listen to the tape, write out the missing information and then make a conversation talking about it.

Hot and Sour Soup(酸辣汤)

Ingredients	Steps of Making Hot and Sour Soup
_____ strips	1. put pork strips, mushrooms, bamboo shoots and ham into boiling water
dried _____	2. heat for several minutes
_____ shoots	3. _____
_____	4. continue to simmer for another few more minutes
boiling _____	5. _____
_____ broth	6. add the well-beaten egg into the soup
shrimp	7. _____
soy sauce	
vinegar	
_____	
black _____	
cornstarch	
_____	
egg	

Activity 5

I. The following are two kinds of soups. Listen to the tape and write out the ingredients for each of them.

Gold Carp and Tofu Soup (鲫鱼豆腐汤)

_____, _____, _____, _____, _____

Egg Drop Soup (蛋花汤)

_____, _____, _____, _____, _____

II. Match the words in column A with those in column B.

A	B
tofu	火腿
dried shrimp	黄瓜
ham	虾米
cucumber	蘑菇
gold carp	香菜
mushroom	豆腐
egg	油菜
laver	紫菜
rape	鲫鱼
coriander	鸡蛋

Learning Tips

Traditional Regional Soups

Ajiaco—A chicken soup from Colombia.

Avgolemono—A Greek chicken soup with lemon and egg.

Bajajou—A soup of Slovakian origin. Ingredients include boiled cow intestines, chicken egg, onion and rice.

Bird's nest soup is a delicacy in Chinese cuisine.

Bisque—A thick, creamy, highly-seasoned and pureed soup of French origin.

Canja de Galinha—A Portuguese soup of chicken, rice and lemon.

Canh chua (sour soup)—A Vietnamese dish made with rice, fish, various vegetables, and in some cases pineapple.

Egg drop soup—A savory Chinese soup made from adding already-beaten eggs into boiling water or broth.

Maryland Crab Soup—A soup made of vegetables, blue crab, and Old Bay Seasoning in a tomato base. From Maryland, United States.

Faki soupa—A Greek soup, with carrots, olive oil, herbs and possibly tomato sauce or vinegar.

Goulash—A Hungarian soup of beef, paprika and onion.

Íslensk Kjötsúpa—Traditional Icelandic meat soup made with lamb and vegetables.

Lan Sikik—A Thai soup made with noodle, dried fish and tomato extract.

Lentil soup—A soup popular in the Middle East and Mediterranean.

Menudo—A traditional Mexican soup with tripe and hominy.

Minestrone—An Italian vegetable soup.

Miso soup—A Japanese soup made from fish broth and fermented soy.

Snert—A thick pea soup, eaten with sliced sausage in the Netherlands.

Shchav—A sorrel soup in Polish, Russian and Yiddish cuisines.

Solyanka—A cabbage soup from Russia.

Tarator—A Bulgarian cold soup made from yogurt and cucumbers.

Zurek—A Polish wheat soup with sausages often served in a bowl made of bread.

Unit 8

Making a Dish

Part A Making Western Food

Teaching hours: 2 hours

LEARNING GOALS

To be able to
* get background information of western food
* get familiar with western food
* tell the amount of ingredients needed
* tell the ways of cooking

VOCABULARY ASSISTANCE

macaroni	n.	通心粉	flour	n.	面粉
spinach	n.	芹菜	cream	n.	奶油
berries	n.	浆果,如:草莓等	poach	v.	温煮
steam	v.	蒸	stew	v.	烩
minced garlic		蒜蓉	grated cheese		奶酪粉
onion chopped		碎洋葱	fresh milk		鲜奶
bay leaves		月桂叶	deep fry		炸
pan fry		煎			

Start You Off

The following is something about western food. Look up the new words in the dictionary and make a conversation talking about western food.

Western food is a term referring to the food of Europe and other Western countries. Western food includes that of Europe and to some extent Russia, as well as non-indigenous food of North America, Australasia, Oceania, and Latin America.

The food of Western countries are diversed by themselves, although there are common characteristics that distinguish western cooking from that of Asian countries. Compared with traditional cooking of Asian countries, for example, meat is more prominent and substantial in serving-size. Steak in particular is a common dish across the West. Similarly to some Asian cuisines, western food also puts emphasis on sauces as condiments and seasonings.

Focus on Language

Listen and write out the missing words.

_____ and _____ cuisines are very appealing to the _____; at the _____ time, they are very stimulating to the _____. The colorful _____ are full of natural _____ and in good _____.

⇨ Language Tips

1. Discussing the amount of ingredients needed

◆ What are we going to make today, chef?
◇ We are going to make an Italian food.
◆ What is it?
◇ Spaghetti with Simmered Shrimps in Curry Sauce.
◆ What ingredients and how much of the ingredients should I prepare?
◇ You have to prepare 160g Spaghetti (cooked), 6 large shrimps, 120g onion (diced), 100g sweet red pepper (diced), 20ml olive oil.
◆ Anything else?
◇ Of course. You still have to prepare 10g butter, 40ml water, 15g curry powder, 0.25tsp salt and 0.25tsp sugar.
◆ Is that all?
◇ Yes. That's all.

Practice 1

Pair-work: Make a conversation talking about the ingredients and amount of ingredients needed for Baked Seafood with Macaroni by using the following tips.

Baked Seafood with Macaroni (焗白汁海鲜通心粉)

Ingredients

100 g salmon, 6 scallops , 4 mussels,

200 g macaroni cooked,

20 g minced garlic, 20 g grated cheese,

100 g onion, chopped,

Ingredients for white sauce

20 g butter, 15 g flour, 70 ml fresh milk,

Seasonings

0.25 tsp salt, 0.25 tsp pepper.

Practice 2

Listen and write out the amount of ingredients.

_____	spinach	_____	onion
_____	bacon	_____	flour
_____	fresh milk	_____	salt
_____	pepper	_____	flour
_____	cream	_____	minced garlic
_____	bay leave		

2. Ways of cooking

◆ What are the ways of cooking western food, chef?
◇ They are more or less the same as we cook Chinese food.
◆ For instance?
◇ Deep-fry, pan-fry, sauté, poach, bake, stew, steam, braise, grill and so on.

Practice 1

Match the words in column A with the definitions in column B.

A	B
1. braise	a. to cook (meat) slowly in fat and a little liquid in a covered dish
2. poach	b. to cook inside the oven
3. steam	c. to cook by allowing steam to heat
4. barbecue	d. to cook quickly in a little hot oil or fat
5. stew	e. to cook (something) slowly and gently in liquid in a closed vessel
6. sauté	f. to cook (meat) on an open fire, usually outdoors
7. bake	g. to cook (esp. eggs or fish) in gently boiling water or other liquid sometimes in a special pan

Practice 2

Listen and write out the different ways of cooking in the proper place according to what you hear from the tape.

_____ tuna fillet	_____ sole fillet and scallop
_____ salmon fillet	_____ stuffed turkey
_____ chicken feet	_____ bacon rolls
_____ beef	_____ lobster with garlic
_____ eel in black bean sauce	_____ egg
_____ lettuce	_____ king prawn

Practice 3

Listen to the tape and write out the missing information.

New Zealand Beef Tenderloin with King Prawn (新西兰牛排配明虾)

Ingredients

_____ tenderloin, _____ prawn, rice, _____ chips
asparagus, _____ juice, curry powder
carrot, _____, morel sauce (羊肚菌汁)
cream of white _____ sauce

Proceed (制作)

Marinate(腌) beef tenderloin with _____ and _____.
Marinate king _____ with lemon juice.
_____ the rice with curry powder, _____ onion and put it on plate.
_____ the beef tenderloin to medium well, _____ it on
the rice and _____ the morel sauce around it.
Pan-fry king prawn and put it _____ the beef tenderloin,
_____ with sautéd vegetables, potato chips, etc.
_____ the cream of _____ wine sauce.

Summarize Key Expressions

1. Discussing the amount of ingredients

   a. How many onions should I prepare, chef?
      You have to prepare 6.
   b. How much flour and olive oil do you need?
      300 g flour and 20 lm olive oil.

   c. What about salt and pepper?
      0.25 tsp salt and 0.30 tsp pepper.
   d. And milk?
      2 cups of milk, please.

2. **Ways of cooking**
   a. What are the ways of cooking western food, chef?
   b. They are more or less the same as we cook Chinese food.
   c. For instance: braise, roast, grill, barbecue, fry, sauté, bake, stew, poach, steam and so on.
   d. Stir-fry the chicken liver with chopped onion until cooked.
   e. Braise /stew/boil the spare ribs for another 15 minutes.
   f. Roast /grill/ bake/ barbecue the turkey.
   g. Deep-fry the lotus roots until ...
   h. Pan-fry the king prawn with lemon juice.
   i. Marinate beef tenderloin with salt and pepper.

Give It a Try

Task 1

Listen and write out the amount of ingredients needed.

_____ lobsters	_____ white wine
_____ salt	_____ large shrimps
_____ water	_____ bay leaves
_____ pork	_____ water

Task 2

Pair-work: Look at the cookery book, find out as many recipes of dishes, soup, salad, cakes etc. as possible and practice talking about the amount of ingredients needed.

Task 3

Group-work: Work in groups and take turns speaking out as many dishes cooked by any of the following means as possible.

| braise | roast | grill | barbecue | fry |
| sauté | bake | stew | poach | steam |

Do Extension Activities

Activity 1

Listen to the tape, write out the ingredients and the amount of ingredients needed for Baked Lobster with Cheese and White Wine Sauce.

Baked Lobster with Cheese and White Wine Sauce

Ingredients	The amount of ingredients needed
l _ _ _ _ _ _	_____ g
o _ _ _ _	_____ g
g _ _ _ _ _	_____ g
m _ _ _ _ _ _ _	_____ g
b _ _ _ _ _	_____ g
f _ _ _ _	_____ g
w _ _ _ _ w _ _ _	_____ ml
f _ _ _ _ m _ _ _	_____ ml
c _ _ _ _	_____ ml
c _ _ _ _ _	_____ g

Activity 2

Listen and match the words in column A with those in column B.

A	B
braise	seasonal vegetables
soft-fry	shrimp meat balls
stir-fry	fish
deep-fry	shrimp with egg
scramble	turkey
steam	giant lobster in black bean sauce
boil	sea cucumber and mushroom
sauté	beef
roast	eggs with tomato
barbecue	chicken wing
bake	black fungus with red pepper

Activity 3

Listen to the tape, write out the missing words and then rearrange the statements into the right order.

Grilled Salmon in Norwegian Style (挪威三文鱼)
- _____ the salmon on plate, serve with the sliced vegetables, potatoes and asparagus.
- _____ the saffron sauce.
- _____ salmon with olive oil to be medium and roast it to be done.
- _____ salmon with salt, pepper, white wine, sliced lemon and oregano.

Activity 4

Translate the following into English.

制作油咖喱，我们需要葱80克、蒜片80克、姜40克、青辣椒60克、红辣椒60克、咖喱粉160克、姜粉40克、辣椒粉20克、白糖80克、香叶2片、油650克。除此之外，我们还需要：盐30克、鸡精2茶匙、生粉15克、水180克、蚝油30克、糖30克、酱油2汤匙。

Activity 5

Look up the new words in the dictionary and translate the following recipe into Chinese.

Frog Leg and Snail in French Style

Ingredients: frog leg, snail, fennel, bread, white wine, brown sauce, mixed herbs, salt and pepper

Proceed: (1) Cook the fennel, season and cut it into fan shape. (2) Fry frog leg and snail, add white wine and brown sauce, then season. (3) Put all ingredients in dish and garnish with roasted bread and mixed herbs.

Activity 6

Listen and answer the following questions.

1. What is very famous in the world?
2. What does French dinner usually start with?
3. What does formal French dinner include?

Learning Tips

French Apéritif

Apéritif time is the important and happy moment when you welcome your guests. You have to show them that you are happy to see them again, as well as help them wait for the next guest to come. So, you can serve a drink to them with a few appetizers and take this moment as an opportunity to introduce them to each other.

Drinks

The greatest and ideal apéritif you can serve is a glass of champagne ; but you have many other options. French people usually offer a choice of classic alcohol, like whisky, or fortified wine (掺了酒精的饭后酒), like Martini.

Appetizers

Again, you have all sorts of options. For instance you can try potato chips or peanuts styled snack or you can have better and healthier options that will look and taste good, like: canapés with typical French spreads, vegetable with special (homemade) dips and other original surprises.

Cooking Measurement Equivalents

The Metric System 公制

Weight 重量

1 kg（千克）= 2 市斤

Capacity 容量

1 L（升）= 1000 ml（毫升）

The British and American System 英美制

Weight 重量

1 lb（磅）= 16 oz（盎司/安士）= 453.6g（克）

1 oz（盎司/安士）= 16 dr.（打兰）= 28.35g（克）

1 dr.（打兰）= 1.771g（克）

Capacity 容量

1 gal（加仑）= 4qt（夸脱）= 4.546 L（升）

1qt（夸脱）= 2 pt（品脱）= 1.1356 L（升）

1pt（品脱）= 4GL（及耳）= 0.5682 L（升）

1GL（及耳）= 5oz（盎司/安士）= 0.142 L（升）

1oz（盎司/安士）= 28.4ml（毫升）

The American System 美制

Capacity 容量

1 gal（加仑）= 4qt（夸脱）

1 qt（夸脱）= 2 pt（品脱）
1 pt（品脱）= 2 cup 杯 = 16 oz（盎司/安士）
1 cup 杯 = 2 GL（及耳）= 8 oz（盎司/安士）
1 GL（及耳）= 8 table spoon（汤匙）= 4 oz（盎司/安士）
1 oz（盎司/安士）= 2 table spoon（汤匙）
1 table spoon（汤匙）= 3 tea spoon（茶匙）= 1/2 oz（盎司/安士）
1 tea spoon（茶匙）= 1/6 oz（盎司/安士）
1 oz（盎司/安士）= 28.4 ml（毫升）

Abbreviations

g 克	kg 千克	L 升	l 毫升
lb 磅	oz 盎司/安士	dr. 打兰	gal 加仑
qt 夸脱	pt 品脱	GL 及耳	table spoon 汤匙
tea spoon 茶匙			

Unit 8

Part B Making Western & Chinese Food

Teaching hours: 2 hours

LEARNING GOALS

To be able to
* get background information of western and Chinese food
* tell the duration of cooking
* tell the process of cooking
* discuss typical food

pizza	n.	比萨	recipe	n.	菜谱
dough	n.	面团	elastic	adj.	有弹性的
preheat	v.	预热	Spaghetti	n.	意大利面
Borscht Moscow Style		莫斯科红菜汤	Chicken Kiev		黄油鸡卷
Goose Liver Pie		鹅肝派	Snails in Shell Herb Butter		焗蜗牛
Caesar Salad		凯撒沙拉	Fried Pork Chop Milanese		米兰煎猪排
Hawaii Seafood Salad		夏威夷海鲜沙拉	Waldorf Salad		华道夫沙拉
London Broil		伦敦杂肉扒	Bird's Nest Soup		燕窝汤
Sour West Lake Fish		西湖醋鱼	Huangshan Braised Pigeon		黄山炖鸽
Mandarin Fish		鳜鱼	Hot Pot		火锅
Roasted Suckling Pig		烤乳猪	Peppery and Hot Chicken		麻辣鸡

Start You Off

Activity 1

Listen to the Table Manners and answer the following questions.

1. What is the main difference between Chinese and western eating habits?
2. How do Chinese hosts show their politeness?
3. What can you do if you feel uncomfortable to eat the food up?

Activity 2

Listen to the Table Manners again and complete the statements.

1. Chinese are very proud of their _____ and will _____ to

show their hospitality.

2. Sometimes the _____ uses his _____ to put food in your bowl or plate. This is a _____ .

3. The appropriate thing _____ would be _____ .

Focus on Language

Listen to the tape and complete the following statements.

1. Chinese cooking is famous for its _____ and _____ .
2. It was the Chinese who invented the technique of making and using _____ _____ _____ and _____ .
3. Every Chinese _____, _____ and _____ has its own characteristics.

⇨ Language Tips

1. Discussing the time needed

◆ What are we going to make today, chef?
◇ We are going to make Pizza, typical Italian food.
◆ I know the recipe. Let me prepare the ingredients.
◇ Ok. Go ahead.
…
◆ Everything is ready. And I have just made the dough.
◇ The dough cannot be used until it is elastic. We have to wait for an hour.
◆ Alright.
◇ Then roll the dough into rounds on the pizza plate. Spread with cheese, filling, other ingredients and more cheese. At last bake it in the moderate oven 180°C for about 15 minutes.
◆ Okay.

Practice 1

Listen and complete the following statements.

1. Roast the chicken for _____ .
2. Sauté the mushroom for _____ .
3. Grill the mutton for _____ .
4. Deep-fry the fish in the hot oil for _____ .
5. Braise the beef for _____ .

Unit 8

Practice 2

Listen and decide whether the following statements are true or false.

1. Bake the bread for about 30 minutes until it turns golden brown.
2. Preheat the oven to 119°C. Bake the skewers for 15 minutes and then serve.
3. Stew the beef for about 14 minutes, then add some water and stew it for another 40 minutes.
4. Boil the egg for 8 minutes and 30 seconds.

2. Discussing typical food

> ◆ Excuse me. Can you tell me what is typical Beijing local specialty?
> ◇ Sure. It is Beijing Roast Duck.
> ◆ What is typical Hunan food?
> ◇ It is Locus Seed with Rock Candy, Hot-spiced and Peppered Fledgling Chicken and Mutton Soup with Tortoise.
> ◆ How about Sichuan food?
> ◇ Sichuan food is very hot and spicy. Mapo Tofu, Fried Diced Chicken with Chili Sauce are typical Sichuan food.

Practice 1

Listen to the tape and match the information.

Russian	Hawaii Seafood Salad
French	Caesar Salad
Italian	Boiled Pork with Sour Cabbage Berlin Style
American	London Broil
English	Chicken Kiev
German	Goose Liver Pie

Practice 2

Pair-work: Find out the typical food of Quanjude, Qiaojiangnan, Huangchenglaoma, Kongyiji, Jinyangfanzhuang, Shaguoju, Kaorouwan and make conversations by using the following patterns.

A: What are the specialties of ...?
B: They are ...
A: And what is the typical food of ...?
B: It is...

Practice 3

Listen to the tape and answer the following questions.

1. Does Chinese cuisine have a long history?
2. What are the eight main regional cuisines?
3. What is the typical food for Cantonese, Hunan and Sichuan cuisine?

Summarize Key Expressions

1. **Discussing the time needed**
   a. Boil the egg for one more minute.
   b. Braise the mutton for another 30 minutes.
   c. Deep-fry the prawns with brown sauce for 8 to 9 minutes.
   d. Sauté the shredded pork in sweet bean sauce for less than 5 minutes.
   e. Stir-fry the mushroom for 3 and a half minute.
   f. Bake the beef in the oven until it's well done.
   g. It doesn't take long to steam the rice, about 7 to 8 minutes.
   h. It takes more than half an hour to roast the chicken.
   i. Barbecue the duck wing for a while.

2. **Talking about specialties**
   a. What is typical Russian food?
      Borscht Moscow style, Chicken Kiev and so on.
   b. How about French, Italian and American food?
      Goose Liver Pie, Snails in Shell Herb Butter are world famous French food; Caesar Salad, Fried Pork Chop Milanese, Spaghetti are well-known Italian food and Hawaii Seafood Salad, Waldorf Salad are typical American food.
   c. And what are the specialties of English and German Food?
      London Broil and Boiled Pork with Sour Cabbage Berlin Style.
   d. What is the local specialty of Mexico?
      It is Taco.
   e. What are the famous Chinese cuisines?
      Famous Chinese cuisines are Cantonese, Fujian, Hunan, Shandong, Sichuan, Huaiyang, Beijing, Shanghai cuisine etc.
   f. Is Beijing Roast Duck a local speciality?
      It sure is.
   g. Can you name some of the typical dishes of Cantonese, Hunan, Sichuan, Shandong, Huaiyang cuisines?

Of course. Roasted Suckling Pig is typical Cantonese cuisine; Hunan cuisine is well-known for its Peppery and Hot Chicken; Sichuan cuisine is famous for its Hot Pot. Fried Sea Cucumber with Fistulous Onion is the specialty of Shandong cuisine; Sweet and Sour Mandarinfish is well-known Huaiyang cuisine.

Give It a Try

Task 1

Pair-work: Look at the cookery book and make conversations talking about the time needed for a dish, a soup, a cake, a barbecue etc.

Task 2

Listen and write out the missing words.

Chinese cuisine _____ from the various regions of China and has become _____ in many other parts of the world —from East _____ to North _____, Australia, Western _____ and Southern _____. There are eight main regional cuisines, Anhui, Cantonese, Fujian, Hunan, Jiangsu, Shandong, Sichuan and Zhejiang. Occasionally _____ cuisine and _____ cuisine are also cited along with the eight regional styles as the _____ (十大菜系).

Task 3

Listen to the conversation, fill in the chart and make a conversation talking about today's special dish.

Today's Specialty:	
How to Prepare:	
first:	
next:	
then:	
after that:	
at last:	

Do Extension Activities

Activity 1

Translate the following into Chinese.

1. Preheat the oven to 200°C. Place the chicken into the oven and bake for 10 to 15 minutes

    and then take it out.

2. When you barbecue the mutton, you should turn it over occasionally.
3. Add 2 cups of water into the pot and steam the fish for another 10 minutes.

Activity 2

Make conversations with your partner talking about typical Beijing cuisine.

Activity 3

Listen to the tape about typical food, complete the following statements and make a conversation talking about Shandong Dishes.

Shandong Dishes

Shandong Cuisine is famous for _____,
_____,
and _____.

The raw material used are mainly d_____ a_____,
b_____, s_____ and v_____.

The masterful cooking techniques include _____,
_____,
_____,
_____ and _____,
using s_____,
and crystallizing with h_____.

Famous Shandong cuisines are _____,
_____,
_____.

The dishes are t_____ and f_____.

Activity 4

Listen to the tape, complete the following statements and use the information given to make a conversation.

Huaiyang Dishes

The three places mentioned are: Y_____, Z_____ and H_____.
The river mentioned is: Y_____ River.

Huaiyang dishes are characterized by: the s _____ in material selection,
the c _____ and f _____ of its ingredients
the f _____ workmanship in c _____, matching,
c _____ and arranging.

The features of the dishes are: l _____,
f _____,
s _____,
mildness of t _____.

Famous Huaiyang dishes are: Crystal _____,
Crisp _____,
Sweet and Sour Mandarinfish.

Activity 5

Read the following passage and do exercises.

Of the world's two great cuisines, the Chinese is, in fact, much older in tradition than the French. There are many Chinese dishes that are well known throughout the world and even though they may not have been tasted by a great many people.

One of the great dishes is Bird's Nest Soup, which is made from the mucus (黏液) from the salivary(分泌唾液的) glands (腺) of the small salangane (金丝燕). It is a soup with fantastic flavor. Shark's Fin Soup is another rare and famous dish. Since the fins are purchased dry, the soup requires a long and careful preparation, only the loose shark's fin is used, and it is prepared with shredded chicken, crabmeat, or pork in chicken stock. The finest and most costly shark's fin soup is a clear one to which no starch is added.

Another world-famous dish is Beijing Roast Duck. It is prepared from a 3-4-month-old Beijing white duck. After being cleaned, the duck is plugged (塞住/堵住) and half filled with water; it is then hooked on a spit in a huge, round doorless oven so that while the water steams the inside of the duck, the outside is roasted over a fire made from wood of the jujube (枣子), pear or apricot (杏) trees. The whole duck is usually brought to the table by the chef and then cut into thin slices. The diner will dip the chopped cucumber and scallion into sweet soybean paste, put them on a small, thin pancake with duck slices, wrap the pancake into a roll and then serve.

Sea cucumbers are also well known to foreign visitors. They are often served with abalone (鲍鱼) or fish maw.

In the famous Mongolian Hot Pot, thinly sliced strips of lamb are cooked in boiling water in a special vessel (容器) attached to a brazier. The lamb strips are picked up with chopsticks and placed in the boiling water, then taken out a few minutes later and served with special sauce. To end the meal, a soup is often prepared with vegetables and noodles and bean curd added to the boiling stock.

Dishes Mentioned

1.
2.
3. Beijing Roast Duck
4.
5.

Steps of Preparing and Serving Beijing Roast Duck

1.
2.
3.
4.
5.
6.
7.

Learning Tips

What Is Italian Cooking?

Many non-Italians identify Italian cooking with a few of its most popular dishes, like pizza and spaghetti. People often express the opinion that Italian cooking is all pretty much alike. However, those who travel through Italy notice differences in eating habits between cities, even those only a few miles apart.

Not only does each region have its own style, but each community and each valley has a different way of cooking as well. Every town has a distinctive way of making sausage, special kinds of cheese and wine, and a local type of bread. If you ask people, even in the same area, how to make pasta sauce, they will all have different answers.

Variations in the omnipresent pasta are another example of the multiplicity of Italian recipes: soft egg noodles in the north, hard-boiled spaghetti in the south, with every conceivable variation in size and shape. Perhaps no other country in the world has a cooking style so finely fragmented into different divisions. So why is Risotto typical of Milan; why did Tortellini originate in Bologna; and why is Pizza so popular in Naples?

This is so for the same reason that Italy has only one unifying Italian language, yet hundreds of different spoken dialects. Italy is a country of great variety, and cooking is just another aspect of the diversity of Italian culture.

Unit 9

Dessert

Part A Making a Dessert I

Teaching hours: 2 hours

LEARNING GOALS

To be able to
- identify common dessert
- know baking equipment
- describe baking equipment's use
- line cake tins
- test cakes
- calculate quantities and cut cakes

VOCABULARY ASSISTANCE

muffin	n.	马粉包	donut	n.	多纳圈
croissant	n.	牛角包	bun	n.	小圆包
tiramisu	n.	提拉米苏	sponge	n.	海绵蛋糕
plait bread		辫包	quick-mix		半成品
balloon whisk		蛋抽	electric hand mixer		电动搅拌器
greaseproof paper		防油纸			

Start You Off

Activity 1

The following pictures show some common dessert. Look at the pictures below and write down the names of them.

烹饪英语

1. _____cake_____ 2. _____ 3. _____ 4. _____

5. _____ 6. _____ 7. _____ 8. _____

9. _____ 10. _____ 11. _____ 12. _____

Activity 2

Look at the pictures below and do the question and answer practice in pairs.

        A: What is it?
        B: It's _____ .

Unit 9

Focus on Language

Listening

Cakes

Listen to the passage and read after it. Then fill in the blanks in the passage and try to find the answers to the questions.

_____(1) are the highlight of many celebrations. What_____(2) recipes would be complete without a cake with candles to blow out, or a_____(3) without a beautiful cake to cut? Some of the most traditional_____(4) provide the best bases for decorating. None of the cakes involve complicated techniques, and several are as simple as putting the ingredients into a bowl, and mixing them together.

_____(5) is one of our most popular special occasion cakes. Among its advantages is that it keeps really well and in fact improves with storage, so it can be baked well ahead of time and_____(6) in easy stages. It also provides a wonderfully firm base for all sorts of elegant or novelty decorations. There are other ideas, too, for those who prefer a less rich tasting cakes, such as the Madeira or a light fruit cake, as well as a quick-mix_____(7) for those last-minute, spontaneous celebrations.

Questions:
1. What are the highlight of many celebrations?
2. In what sort of celebration party do we often use a cake?
3. What is one of our most popular special occasion cakes?

➡ Language Tips

1. Usage of baking equipment

◆ Could you (please) tell me what a sieve is used for?
◇ It is for sifting icing sugar.
◆ Could(Shall) I sift the flour with a sieve?
◇ Sure. Go ahead.

Practice 1

Look at the table below, follow the way in "Usage of baking equipment" and make two-sentence conversations in pairs.

Baking Items	Usage
Scales	precise measuring
Bowls	mixing
Balloon whisks	beating egg or cream mixtures
Spatulas	scraping
Oven gloves	removing anything hot from the oven
Cake tin	preventing the cake which will be overcooked

Practice 2

Role-play the conversation given below and try to know the basic equipment for cake making.

Commis: Good morning, chef.
Chef: Good morning.
Commis: What are we going to prepare today?
Chef: Making a cake. Would you like to give me a hand?
Commis: Sure.
Chef: Bring me a cake board, please.
Commis: OK. Chef, there are many cake boards in different size. Which one do you want?
Chef: The largest one, please.
Commis: Chef, we'll choose the shape and size to fit the cake, is that right?
Chef: Exactly. Thick boards are for large, heavy cakes, royal iced cakes and any other fruit cakes coated in icing. The board should be 5 cm larger than the size for the cake. Thinner boards are for small Madeira cakes and other lighter cakes covered with icing such as butter, glace or fudge. There can be about 2.5 cm larger than the cake size.
Commis: I got it. Thank you.

Practice 3

Work in pairs. Go over the model expressions in "Usage of baking equipment" and make short conversations with the information given below.

Here is the information you need:

> Measuring Jug:
> A measuring jug is easy to read and means liquids are calculated accurately.
>
> Measuring Spoons:
> These are available in a standard size, making the measuring of small amounts more accurate.
>
> Greaseproof Paper:
> Used to line cake tins to prevent cakes from sticking.
>
> Wooden / Metal Spoons:
> Wooden spoons in various sizes are essential for beating mixtures together when not using an electric mixer, while metal spoons are necessary for folding in ingredients and for smoothing over mixtures to give a flat surface before baking.

2. Lining Cake Tins

Practice 1

Lining Cake Tins

Fill in the blanks with the words that you will hear on the tape.

Greaseproof paper is normally used for _____ (1). The paper lining prevents the cakes from _____ (2) to the tins and makes them easier to _____ (3). Different cake recipes require slightly different techniques of linings, depending on the _____ (4) of the tin, the type of cake mixture, and how long the cake needs to cook. _____ (5) sponge cakes require only one _____ (6) of paper to line the base, for example, whereas _____ (7) fruit cakes that often bake for several hours if they are large in size need to be lined with a double layer of paper on the _____ (8) and sides. This extra protection also helps cakes to cook evenly.

Practice 2

Role-play the conversation given below and learn how to line a shallow round tin.

Chef: Now, let me tell you the first technique for cake making.
Commis: Lining a round tin, right?

Chef: Yes. First, put the tin on a piece of greaseproof paper and draw around the base of the tin. And cut out the circle just inside the marked line.

Commis: OK, let me have a try.

Chef: Good. Next, brush the inside of the tin lightly with a little vegetable oil and position the paper circle in the base of the tin. Brush the paper with a little more vegetable oil.

Commis: Chef, can I use softened butter or margarine in place of vegetable oil?

Chef: Yes, you can.

Practice 3

Rearrange the following statements according to the right order of lining a deep round cake tin.

(   ) For the sides of the tin, cut out a double thickness strip of greaseproof paper that will wrap around the outside of the tin, allowing a slight overlap which is 2.5 cm taller than the depth of the tin.

(   ) Brush the inside of the tin with vegetable oil. Slip the side lining into the tin so the snipped edge fits into the curve of the base and sits flat.

(   ) Put the tin on a double thickness of greaseproof paper and draw around the base. Cut out just inside the line.

(   ) Fold over 2.5 cm along the length of the side lining. Snip the paper along its length, inside the fold, at short intervals.

(   ) Position the base lining in the tin and brush the paper with a little more vegetable oil.

Summarize Key Expressions

1. **Asking the name of baking equipment**
   a. What is this?
   b. What is that?
   c. What is it?
   d. What is the name of the item?

2. **Giving an answer**
   a. This is a metal spoon.
   b. That is a wire rack.
   c. It is a cake board.

3. **Asking about the use of baking equipment**
   a. What is a balloon whisk for?

b. What is a scale used for?

c. Shall I sift the flour with a sieve?

4. **Asking for help**

a. Would you like to give me a hand?

b. Could you help me?

c. Please bring me a mixing bowl.

d. Fetch the pastry brush, please.

e. Please give me the oven gloves.

Give It a Try

Task 1

Role-play the following short conversation and make new conversations with the words given below.

Chef: Hand me a sieve.
Commis: Here you are. What is a sieve used for?
Chef: It is used for sifting icing sugar.
         (a flour sieve, flour; a bowl, mixing; electric whisks, beating egg whites)

Task 2

Ask and answer the following questions with your partner by using a complete sentence.

1. What is a cake board for?
2. Shall I measure the milk with the measuring jug?
3. Who hands the chef a cake tin?
4. Could I use the spatulas to scrape the cake?
5. Who asks the commis to sift the icing sugar?

Do Extension Activities

Activity 1

Read the passage aloud and write down the key points in every paragraph.

Testing Cakes

▲ Always check the cake 5–10 minutes before the given cooking time is completed, just in case the oven is a little fast. It is always better to undercook a cake slightly, since the

mixture continues to cook in the tin after removing it from the oven.
Key points: _____
_____

▲ Always test the cake immediately before removing it from the oven, just in case it is not ready at the advised time. This could be due to a slow oven.
Key points: _____
_____

▲ For all cakes, other than fruit cakes, test by pressing very lightly on the centre of the cake with fingers; if it springs back, the cake is cooked. Otherwise your fingers will leave a slight depression, indicating that the cake needs extra cooking time. Retest at 5-minute intervals.
Key points: _____
_____

▲ Fruit cakes are best tested using a warmed skewer inserted into the centre of the cake. If the skewer comes out clean, the cake is ready. Otherwise return the cake to the oven and retest at 10-minute intervals.
Key points: _____
_____

Learning Tips

Calculating Quantities and Cutting Cakes

To work out the number of servings from a round or square cake is extremely simple and the final total depends on whether you require just a small finger of cake or a more substantial slice.

Whether the cake is round or square, cut across the cake from edge to edge into about 2.5 cm slices, thinner if desired. Cut each slice into 5 cm pieces or thereabouts.

Using these guidelines, it should be easy to calculate the number of cake slices you can cut from any given size cake. A square cake is larger than a round cake of the same proportions and will yield more slices. On a round cake the slices become smaller at the curved edges, and the first and last slice of the cake is mainly marzipan and icing. Always keep this in mind when calculating the servings.

Unit 9

Part B Making a Dessert II

Teaching hours: 2 hours

LEARNING GOALS

To be able to
- identify traditional cakes
- identify icing equipment
- make royal icing
- decorate with chocolate
- read recipe and directions

VOCABULARY ASSISTANCE

gateau	n.	奶油蛋糕	panforte	n.	意大利果包
classic	n. & adj.	经典的	turntable	n.	转台
swirl	n.	旋涡状	glyceriner	n.	甘油
damp	adj.	湿润的	foil	n.	锡纸
tsp = table spoon		茶匙	Madeira cake		马德拉蛋糕
piping nozzle		挤嘴	saturated fat		饱和脂肪

Start You Off

Activity 1

The following pictures show some well-known and traditional cakes. Look at the pictures below and write down the names of them.

1. _____   2. _____   3. _____

4._____   5._____   6._____

7._____   8._____   9._____

Activity 2

Look at the icing equipment below and do the question and answer practice in pairs.

A: What is it?
B: It's _____.

Focus on Language

Listening

Listen to the sentences carefully. Complete the following sentences.

1. Sachertorte, one of the world's finest—and most famous—cakes, is a _____ and delectable _____ cake. It often serves in_____ for afternoon tea.

2. This fruit cake is made without _____, yet retains the _____, familiar _____ of traditional fruit cakes.
3. A rich, _____, American-style cheesecake, baked on a sweet biscuit base. It is topped with a selection of exotic _____; varies the _____ to suit the season.
4. Panforte is a specialty of Siena in Italy, where it is traditionally baked at Christmas. It is a combination of _____ candied peel and _____, which are mixed with sugar _____ before baking.
5. Angel food cake is a true American _____. Although similar to a whisked sponge cake, it differs in that it contains no _____. This results in a delicate _____ texture.

➪ Language Tips

1. Usage of baking equipment

◆ Hand me a flower nail, please.
◇ Here you are. What is a flower nail for?
◆ It is used as a support when piping flowers.

◆ What do you want?
◇ I need an icing turntable.
◆ Why?
◇ Because it revolves, it is particularly handy for piping, or for icing the sides of a round cake with royal icing.

Practice 1

Look at the table below. Follow the way in "Usage of baking equipment" and make two-sentence conversations in pairs.

Decorating equipment	Usage
Plastic scrapers	Giving a smooth or patterned surface to the sides or tops of cakes coated with royal, butter or fudge icing
Paintbrushes	Painting designs on to cakes, adding highlights to flowers or modeled shapes
Greaseproof paper	Making piping bags and drying sugar-frosted flowers and fruits

Practice 2

Role-play the conversation given below for Royal Icing. Take turns and do it.

Commis: Chef, I read it from a book that royal icing gains a regal position in the world of icing. Any special occasion cake which demands a classical, professional finish uses this smooth, satin-like icing. Would you show me how to make it?

Chef: That's just your today's job. This recipe makes it sufficient to cover the top and sides of an 18 cm round or 15 cm square cake.

Commis: OK, I prepare for the ingredients. Ur... 3 egg whites, 6 cups of icing sugar, $1\frac{1}{2}$ tsp glycerine.

Chef: Firstput the egg whites in a bowl and stir lightly with a wooden spoon to break then up.

Commis: Chef, do I sift the icing sugar to get rid of the lumps?

Chef: Yes, you do. Good boy. Next is...

Commis: Add the icing sugar gradually in small quantities, beating well between each addition. Add sufficient icing sugar to make a smooth, white, shiny icing with the consistency of very stiff meringue.

Chef: The meringue should be thin enough to spread, but thick enough to hold its shape. Well, now, beat in the glycerine and lemon juice.

Commis: Why Lemon juice?

Chef: A little lemon juice is added to prevent the icing from discoloring, but too much will make the icing become hard.

Commis: I got it.

Chef: The last step is to let the icing sit for about 1 hour before using. Cover the surface with a piece of damp clear film or a lid so the icing doesn't dry out. Before using, stir the icing to burst any air bubbles. Even when working with royal icing, always keep it covered. Remember?

Commis: Yes, sir.

Chef: You did good job, man.

Commis: Thank you, sir.

Practice 3

Work in pairs. Go over the model expressions in "Usage of baking equipment" and make short conversations with the information given below.

Here is the information you need

American Frosting

This American frosting may be swirled or peaked in a soft coating. It looks perfect as a snowy landscape for Christmas cake.

1. Place the egg white, water, golden syrup and cream of tartar in a heatproof bowl. Whisk together until thoroughly blended.

2. Stir the icing sugar into the mixture and place the bowl over a saucepan of simmering water. Whisk until the mixture becomes thick and white and holds soft peaks.

3. Remove the bowl from the saucepan and continue to whisk the mixture stands up in soft peaks.
4. Use immediately to fill or cover the cake. Once iced, the cake can be decorated in any way you like.

2. Decorating with chocolate

Practice 1

Work in pairs. Go over the model expressions above and make short conversations with the information given below.

Melting
1. Break the chocolate into small pieces and place in a bowl set over a pan of hot water. Be careful not to let water or steam near the chocolate or it will become too thick.
2. When the chocolate is completely melted, remove the pan from the heat and stir.

Coating cakes
1. Stand the cake on a wire rack. It is a good idea to place a sheet of greaseproof paper or a baking sheet underneath the rack to catch any chocolate drips. Pour the chocolate icing over the cake quickly, in one smooth motion, to coat the top and sides.
2. Use a palette knife to smooth the chocolate over the sides, if necessary. Allow the chocolate to set, and then coat with another layer, if wished.

Practice 2

Fill in the blanks with the word that you will hear on the tape.

_____(1)___ decorations can look particularly interesting if different kinds of chocolate—dark, milk and white—are used in combination. White chocolate can be colored, but make sure you use_____(2)__ food coloring for this as_____(3) colorings will thicken it. Store chocolate decorations in the refrigerator in a_____(4) between layers of greaseproof paper until_____(5) . Also, handle the decorations as little as possible with your fingers, as they will leave dull marks on the shiny surface of the chocolate.

3. Making black forest cake

Practice 1

Read the recipe, and prepare all the ingredients in kitchen.

2 eggs
$2^{1}/_{2}$ cups of flour
$2^{1}/_{4}$ cups of sugar
$1^{1}/_{2}$ teaspoons of baking soda
1 teaspoon of salt
$^{1}/_{4}$ teaspoon of baking powder
$1^{1}/_{4}$ cups of water
$^{3}/_{4}$ cup of shortening
1 teaspoon of vanilla
1 bar of sweet chocolate
2 cups of chilled whipping cream
Maraschino cherries
Cherry filling
Sifted icing sugar(optional)

Practice 2

Role-play the conversation given below for Black Forest Cake Making. Take turns to do it.

Commis: I will preheat the oven to 180°C.
Chef: Grease and flour two cake pans.
Commis: I already greased and floured the cake pans.
Chef: Put the flour, sugar, cocoa, baking soda, salt, baking powder, water, shortening, eggs and vanilla in the mixer.
Commis: Shall I mix the ingredients at low speed?
Chef: Yes. For 30 seconds.
Commis: And now?
Chef: Mix the ingredients at high speed.
Commis: For how long?
Chef: For 3 minutes.
(After 3 minutes)
Commis: I will pour the ingredients into the baking pans.
Chef: OK. Put the two pans in the oven.
Commis: For how long?
Chef: 30 minutes approximately.

Commis: And in the meantime?

Chef: prepare the cherry filling.

(After 31 minutes)

Commis: The cake is ready.

Chef: Put the cake on wire racks to cool.

Commis: OK.

(After the cakes have cooled)

Commis: The cakes have cooled. I will spread the whipping cream, cherry filling and frosting.

Chef: Garnish with chocolate curls and Maraschino cherries.

Commis: Shall I refrigerate the cake?

Chef: Of course.

Summarize Key Expressions

1. Asking the oven's temperature

    a. How many degrees Centigrade shall I preheat the oven?

    b. How about the temperature?

    c. What is the temperature?

    d. How many degrees Fahrenheit?

2. Asking for speed

    a. Shall I mix the ingredients at low speed?

    b. No, at high speed.

    c. Beat the eggs and sugar at medium speed.

3. Asking for next step

    a. And in the meantime?

    b. What shall I do now?

    c. What next?

    d. What is next step?

    e. What now?

4. Decorating a cake

    a. Garnish the cake with chocolate curls.

    b. Garnish the cake with Maraschino cherries.

    c. Garnish the cake with whole cherries.

    d. Garnish the cake with pitted cherries.

5. Telling the finished dessert
   a. The cake is ready.
   b. The cake is done.
   c. The cake is firm.
   d. The cake is baked.

Give It a Try

Task 1

Match the phrases in Column A with kitchen equipments in Column B.

A	B
decorate the cake	chocolate comb
divide the cake	cake rack
cool the cake	cake mould
mould the cake	pastry syringe
comb the cake	cake divider

Task 2

Complete the following sentences with proper verbs.

1. _____ the flour, sugar and lemon rind together.
2. _____ the bread with paintbrush.
3. _____ whip cream _____ the banana split.
4. _____ the cake.
5. _____ the cake _____ ten portions.

Do Extension Activities

Activity 1

Read the recipe and directions given below and make a conversations in pairs.

Swiss Roll

Ingredients:
3 eggs
115 g caster sugar
115g plain flour
1tsp baking powder

Directions:

1. Preheat the oven to 180°C. Grease a 33×23 cm Swiss roll tin, line with greaseproof paper and grease the paper.
2. Whisk the egg whites in a clean, dry bowl until stiff. Beat in 2 tbsp of the sugar.
3. Place the egg yolks, remaining sugar and 1 tbsp water in a bowl and beat for about 2 minutes until the mixture is pale and leaves a thick trail when the beaters are lifted.
4. Carefully fold the beaten egg yolks into the egg white mixture with a metal spoon.
5. Sift together the flour and baking powder. Carefully fold the flour mixture into the egg mixture with a metal spoon.
6. Pour the cake mixture into the prepared tin and then smooth the surface, being careful not to press out any air.
7. Bake in the centre of the oven for 12—15 minutes. To test if cooked, press lightly in the center. If the cake springs back it is done. It will also start to come away from the edges of the tin.
8. Turn the cake out on to a piece of greaseproof paper lightly sprinkled with caster sugar. Peel off the lining paper and cut off any crisp edges of the cake with a sharp knife. Spread with jam, if wished, and roll up, using the greaseproof paper as a guide. Leave to cool on a wire rack.

Tip: Swiss rolls do not keep well, so if possible bake on the day of eating. Otherwise, wrap in clear film or foil and store in an airtight container overnight or freeze for up to 3 months.

Learning Tips

Nian Gao: Chinese New Year Cake

Nian Gao is also known as Sticky Cake. This New Year's dish is traditionally fed to the Chinese Kitchen God, so that he will give a favorable report on the family's behavior throughout the previous year when he returns to heaven.

Chinese people like the traditional dessert. They often steam the cake over medium-high to high heat for 45 minutes, or until the edges of the cake pull away from the pan. Remove the cake from the heat and cool. They can also pan-fry the cake, dipping the cake slices in an egg wash before frying. Use a small amount of oil so that the cake will not taste oily. Heat the oil on medium-high to high heat, and then turn the heat down to medium and brown the cake slices briefly on both sides.

Unit 10

Food Safety

Part A Food Contamination

Teaching hours: 2 hours

LEARNING GOALS

To be able to
* identify rodents and insects in kitchen
* know basic operating system in kitchen
* know personal hygiene standards
* understand affecting bacterial reproduction factors
* classify foodborne diseases

VOCABULARY ASSISTANCE

rodent	n.	啮齿类动物	cockroach	n.	蟑螂
hygiene	n.	卫生	microorganism	n.	微生物
pathogenic	adj.	病原的	infection	n.	感染
toxication	n.	中毒	gastrointestinal	adj.	肠胃的
fungi	n.	真菌	symptom	v.	症状
nausea	v.	恶心	cramp	n.	绞痛
hazardous	adj.	危险的			

Start You Off

Activity 1

The following pictures show rodents and insects in kitchen. Look at the pictures below and write down the names of them.

1 _____   2 _____   3 _____   4 _____

Activity 2

A kitchen can be thought of as a system of basic operating activities. Match the words in column A with the phrases in column B.

A	B
Preparing	is a critical control point particularly in food service operations that prepare products well in advance of service
Cooking	is the series of activities performed on food products before cooking.
Holding	is the point at which heat is applied to food to change its color, odor, etc.

Focus on Language

Listening

Listen to the tape and fill in the blanks with the words you will hear on the tape.

Personal Hygiene Standards

All production staff members should wear _____(1) and preferably change into them when they report to work. They should wear hair restraints such as _____(2) , _____(3) , or _____(4). Smoking and eating should be prohibited in food preparation areas. The _____(5) products is periodically necessary, but this must be done in a sanitary way. Utensils used for tasting should never be re-introduced to food products, and no one should use fingers to sample food. _____(6) is critical before, during, and after food preparation activities. _____(7) should be worn when appropriate. Finally, _____(8) shouldn't be allowed in the food preparation area.

Language Tip

1. Food contamination

◆ What is the problem?
◇ There are rats in the kitchen.
◆ What shall I do?
◇ Kill them.

Practice 1

Look at the table below, follow the way in "Food Contamination" and make two-sentences conversations in pairs.

rodents	trap
mice	
insects	kill
cockroches	poison
flies	spray

Practice 2

Ask and answer the following questions with your partner by using a complete sentence.

1. Are there any rodents and insects in your kitchen?
2. How do you know that?
3. What are you going to do with them?
4. How shall we kill them?

2. Factors affecting bacterial reproduction

◆ what does TDZ mean?
◇ TDZ means temperature danger zone.

Practice

Read the passage aloud and answer the following questions.

　　Factors affecting bacterial reproduction include moisture, oxygen level, PH level, time, and temperature factors. All bacteria need moisture in a usable form to grow and reproduce. The amount of water in a food product can be reduced by adding sugar or salt, drying, or freezing.

Oxygen requirements vary based on the species of bacteria. Microorganisms generally reproduce best in food products with a pH between 6.6 and 7.5. Fluctuating temperatures may favor food spoilage and/or the proliferation of foodborne illness microbes. Microorganisms may be classified by the temperature conditions in which they thrive. Storage of raw ingredients influences later bacterial activity, so storage at intermediate temperatures must be kept to a minimum. Because most pathogenic activity takes place in the temperature danger zone (TDZ), food should spend minimal time in this range during storage, preparation, and serving.

1. What factors affect bacterial reproduction?

2. What method can we use to reduce the amount of water in food?

3. What is a PH range that microorganisms reproduce best?

3. Foodborne infections and intoxications

◆ What are the two general types of foodborne diseases?
◇ They are infections and poisonings.

Practice 1

Two commises are discussing their training course on foodborne infections and intoxications. Read the conversation aloud. Act it in pairs.

Commis A: Let's review the food diseases together. Chef said there is a quiz tomorrow. A questions for you first. What are the two general types of foodborne diseases?

Commis B: That's a piece of cake. Infections and poisonings. Your turn. What is infections?

Commis A: Ur... Infections are caused by bacteria and viruses that are transmitted in food and later reproduce inside the body. They invade the gastrointestinal system of humans and may affect other organs. Your turn, what does poisoning mean?

Commis B: Poisonings result from the ingestion of harmful chemicals, poisonous plants or animals, or food contaminated with the poisonous waste products of toxigenic bacteria or fungi. Illnesses that are caused by poisonous plants or animals or toxin-contaminated food are called intoxications.

Commis A: Good boy. Now, tell me their symptoms.

Commis B: Both infections and microbial intoxications produce similar symptoms: nausea, vomiting, intestinal cramps, and diarrhoea. However, micro-bial intoxications usually cause symptoms more quickly than infections.

Commis A: Perfect answer.

Practice 2

Fill in the chart according to the conversation given in Practice 1.

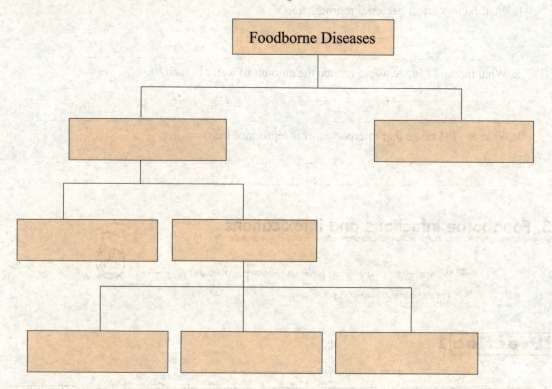

Summarize Key Expressions

1. Talking about the rodents and insects in the kitchen
   a. Is this a rat?
   b. There are mice in the kitchen.
   c. There are cockroaches in the drawers.
   d. There are flies in the kitchen.

2. Telling about the effective methods to kill rodents and insects in the kitchen
   a. Poison rodents and insects.
   b. Trap rodents.
   c. Spray insects.

Give It a Try

Task 1

Read the passage aloud and try to get the ideas about control point.

Control Point

A kitchen can be thought of as a system of basic operating activities or control points. Each control point is a miniature system with its own recognizable structure and functions. Food safety depends on the success of each of these interrelated activities.

Preparing is the series of activities performed on food products before cooking. The preparing function is crucial to quality and cost control. Food preparation mistakes can be irreversible and costly. Some items are riskier than others and must be handled very carefully. They include:

- Potentially hazardous foods
- Foods that possess natural contaminants
- Foods that are susceptible to cross-contamination because they are handled a great deal
- Foods that have multiple preparation steps
- Foods that are exposed to kitchen temperatures(TDZ) for long periods of time
- Foods that have gone through a number of temperature changes
- Foods that are prepared in large quantities

Cooking is the point at which heat is applied to food to change its color, odor, texture, taste, appearance, and nutritional value.

Holding is a critical control point, particularly in food service operations that prepare products well in advance of service. Menu items may be held hot or cold. Holding times should be as short as possible to maintain product quality and reduce food safety hazards. Holding temperatures must also be monitored carefully.

Task 2

Ask and answer the following questions with your partner.

1. What is preparing activities in kitchen?

_____

_____

2. What sorts of foods possess natural contaminants?

_____

3. What is cooking and holding?

_____
_____
_____
_____

Do Extension Activities

Activity 1

Listen to the passage. Fill in the blanks with the words that you will hear on the tape.

Pests such as _____(1) and _____(2) in kitchen are often just a nuisance; however, some can damage _____(3) or possessions in your kitchen. Simple _____(4) measures can stop most problems before they begin. Even when pests do get into kitchen, there is rarely a need to use _____(5). Simply removing their _____(6) and _____(7) is often the most effective control.

Steps such as managing _____(8) so that it attracts fewer insects and animals, _____(9) spilled food, and eliminating _____(10) conditions around the house are simple deterrents. It is good way to get rid of insects and rodents with a minimal amount of risk to health and the environment.

Learning Tips

Control Methods of Insects

Sticky Traps

Flypapers are widely available and effective at trapping flies, especially after a few have been caught on the strip.

Light Traps and Ultrasonic Devices

These devices are designed for use in kitchen, restaurants, dairies and industrial buildings.

Overwintering Insects in the House Structure

For insects trying to enter your kitchen for winter shelter, the best method of preventing a pest problem is to seal up any small holes or cracks before mid to late summer, when they start looking for a way into your house. Repair or replace any damaged screens on windows and doors. Finally, pay particular attention to the south and southwest sides of your kitchen, which can attract more flies because they are warmer.

Part B Food Spoilage and Preservation

Teaching hours: 2 hours

LEARNING GOALS

To be able to
* list the causes of food spoilage
* know preservation methods
* know the characteristics of each category of food

VOCABULARY ASSISTANCE

slaughter	n.	宰杀	segregate	v.	隔离
excessive	adj.	过多的	sanitation	n.	公共卫生
organic	adj.	有机的	dairy	n.	乳制品
radiation	n.	放射			

Start You Off

Activity 1

Listen to the passage carefully. Fill in the blanks with what you will hear.

Almost all food products are composed largely of organic material. Once the food is harvested or slaughtered, the organic material in it begins to _____(1) chemically. Spoilage organisms break down the complex organic substances in foods into their simple and inorganic components. This process is responsible for the changes in the _____ ___(2) , ___(3) , _____(4) , _____(5) , and _____(6) of food products which indicate spoilage. Spoiled food is unfit for human consumption.

The spoilage of food products in a food establishment is often linked to one or more of the following causes:

- Improper storage _____(7)
- Incorrect or excessive storage _____(8)
- Failure to segregate foods in storage
- _____(9) between the receiving and storing of food products
- Inadequate or unacceptable _____(10) resulting in exposure of food products to contaminants

As this list suggests, most food spoilage occurs when foods are at the storing control points. Storage area standards must be designed to prevent or minimize food spoilage and exposure of food products to pathogenic organisms.

Activity 2

Discuss the problems of food poisoning in pairs.

1. What is almost all food composed of?
2. What causes lead to food spoilage?
3. How do we prevent food spoilage?

Focus on Language

Conversation

Role-play conversation below.

Commis: What foods are most dangerous?
Chef: Protein foods: meat, poultry, eggs fish, dairy products, etc.
Commis: Does food poisoning have special taste, special smell or special color?
Chef: No.
Commis: How can I stop food poisoning?
Chef: Refrigerate food below 4° C.
Commis: Is there anything else I should know?
Chef: Never leave food outside the refrigerator for more than two hours.

⇨Language Tips

1. Food poisoning

◆ How do microbes(bacteria) get in food?
◇ Mostly from your hands.
◆ Yes. Everything in the kitchen should be sanitized.
◇ Right. I'll use an antiseptic to sanitize.

Practice 1

Ask and answer the following questions with your partner, using a complete sentence.

1. How do bacteria get in food? Can you give more reasons?
2. Why should everything in the kitchen be sanitized?

3. Does food poisoning have a special taste, special smell or special color?
4. Why should we refrigerate food below 4°C?
5. Can we leave food outside the refrigerator for more than two hours? Why?
6. Do you think that it is important for us to keep the kitchen clean? Why?

Practice 2

Discuss the problems of food poisoning in pairs.

1. How do microbes get in food?
2. What foods are most dangerous? Why?
3. How can we stop food poisoning?

Practice 3

Complete the following sentences with a proper word and then read them aloud.

1. How do microbes get _____ food?
2. Mostly _____ your hands.
3. Everything _____ the kitchen should be sanitized.
4. Watch _____ ! It's dangerous.

2. Food preservation

◇ Storage temperatures of wholesale cuts for beef is 1 to 2 °C.
◆ Humidity of portion cuts for beef is 85%.
◇ Storage time of ground beef is 1 to 2 days.

Practice 1

Look at the following form and try to get the ideas about storage conditions for fresh and frozen meats.
Recommended Storage Conditions for Fresh and Frozen Meats

Products	Storage Temperatures	Relative Humidity (%)	Storage Time
Refrigerated Storage			
Beef			
Wholesale Cuts	1 to 2°C	85	1—2 weeks
Portion Cuts	1 to 2°C	85	4—6 days
Ground Beef	1 to 2°C	85	1—2 days

续表

Pork			
Wholesale Cuts	1 to 2°C	85	5 days
Portion Cuts	1 to 2°C	85	3 days
Ground Pork	1 to 2°C	85	1—2 days
Lamb			
Wholesale Cuts	1 to 2°C	85	1 week
Portion Cuts	1 to 2°C	85	3—4 days
Veal			
Wholesale Cuts	1 to 2°C	90	5 days
Portion Cuts	1 to 2°C	90	3 days
Cured Meats	1 to 2°C	75	2 weeks
Variety Meats	1 to 2°C	85	3—5 days
Freezer Storage			
Beef			
Wholesale Cuts	-23 to -18°C	-	6—10 months
Portion Cuts	-23 to -18°C	-	4—8 months
Ground Beef	-23 to -18°C	-	4—6 months
Pork			
Wholesale Cuts	-23 to -18°C	-	4—8 months
Portion Cuts	-23 to -18°C	-	2—6 months
Ground Pork	-23 to -18°C	-	1—2 months
Lamb			
Wholesale Cuts	-23 to -18°C	-	6—10 months
Portion Cuts	-23 to -18°C	-	4—8 months
Veal			
Wholesale Cuts	-23 to -18°C	-	4—8 months
Portion Cuts	-23 to -18°C	-	2—6 months

Practice 2

The following items indicate the recommended storage, temperatures, and time for food product categories. Remember and use it to finish the tasks below.

Here is the information you need.

Product	Storage Temperatures	Relative Humidity (%)	Storage Time
Refrigerated Storage			
shell eggs	-2 to 2°C	80—85	2—4 weeks
dried eggs	2 °C	minimum	6—12 months
reconstituted eggs	-2 to 2°C	80—85	2—4 weeks
butter	0 to 2°C	85	2—4 weeks
cheese, hard	3 to 4°C	75	4—6 months
cheese, soft	3 to 4°C	75	13—14 days

续表

fluid milk	2 to 3°C	85	6—14 days
reconstituted dried milk	2 to 3°C	85	5—8 days
apples	-1 to 0°C	85	2—6 months
grapefruits	0 to 7°C	85	1—2 months
lemons	8 to 10°C	85	1—4 months
limes	8 to 10°C	85	1—2 months
melons	4 to 7°C	85	2—4 weeks
oranges	0 to 2°C	85	2—3 months
peaches	-1 to 0°C	85	2—4 weeks
berries	-1 to 0°C	85	1—2 weeks
grapes	-1 to 0°C	85	1—2 months
strawberries	-1 to 0°C	85	4—8 days
asparagus	0 to 1°C	90	2—4 weeks
beans	4 to 7°C	85	7—10 days
cabbage	0 to 1°C	90	2—3 months
carrots	0 to 1°C	90	1—3 weeks
cauliflower	0 to 1°C	85	2—3 weeks
corn	-1 to 0°C	85	4—7 days
cucumbers	7 to 9°C	90	1—2 weeks
lettuce	0 to 1°C	90	2—4 weeks
onions	0 to 1°C	75	5—8 months
potatoes	10 to 13°C	85	2—4 months
spinach	0 to 1°C	90	1—2 weeks
squash, zucchini	0 to 2°C	85	1—2 weeks
tomatoes, ripe	0 to 1°C	85	7—10 days
canned vegetables	10 to 21°C	50—60	8—12 months
frozen vegetables	-23 to -18°C		6—10 months
canned fruits	10-22°C	50—60	8—12 months
rozen fruits	-23 to -18°C		6—12 months
Freezer Storage			
whole eggs	-23 to -18°C		6—8 months
ice cream and frozen desserts	-18 to -12°C		2—4 months
Dry Storage			
condensed milk	10 to 21°C	50—60	2—4 months
evaporated milk	10 to 21°C	50—60	8—10 months
dried milk	10 to 21°C	50—60	8—10 months

Summarize Key Expressions

Asking about food poisoning

a. How can we stop food poisoning?
b. How do microbes get in food?
c. How do bacteria get in food?
d. What foods are most dangerous?

Give It a Try

Fill in the form below using the information provided in Practice 2 in "Food Preservation."

Task 1

Recommended Storage Conditions for Fresh and Frozen Eggs

Products	Storage Temperatures	Relative Humidity (%)	Storage Time
Refrigerated Storage			
Freezer Storage			

Unit 10

Task 2

Make a discussion and fill in the following form in pairs.

Recommended Storage Conditions for Dairy Products

Products	Storage Temperatures	Relative Humidity (%)	Storage Time
Refrigerated Storage			
Freezer Storage			
Dry Storage			

Do Extension Activities

Fill in the form below using the information provided in Practice 2 in "Food Preservation."

Activity 1

Recommended Storage Conditions for Fruits

Products	Storage Temperatures	Relative Humidity (%)	Storage Time
Fresh Fruits			
Canned Fruits			
Frozen Fruits			

Activity 2

Fill in the following form.

Recommended Storage Conditions for Vegetables

Products	Storage Temperatures	Relative Humidity (%)	Storage Time
Fresh Vegetables			
Canned Vegetables			
Frozen Vegetables			

Learning Tips

Food Preservation

There are four main objectives of food preservation. Some preservation methods are designed to lengthen the lag phase of bacterial growth. Another objective of food preservation is to delay undesirable autolysis. This is achieved by destroying enzymes or preventing enzymatic action. The third objective is to minimize the damage caused by insects, rodents, and physical trauma. The fourth objective, the prevention of microbiological breakdown of food, is probably the most important. All methods of food preservation are designed to achieve one or more of these objectives.

Vocabulary

A

aboyeur *n.* 〔法〕跑堂喊菜的人	Unit 1 Part A
accessible *adj.* 可进入的	Unit 2 Part A
add *v.* 加入	Unit 3 Part B
anisette *n.* 茴香酒	Unit 3 Part B
appetizer *n.* 开胃菜	Unit 7 Part A
apple *n.* 苹果	Unit 7 Part A
apprentice *n.* 徒弟,学徒工	Unit 1 Part B
appropriate *adj.* 合适的,恰当的	Unit 3 Part B
apricot *n.* 杏	Unit 5 Part A
aprika *n.* 甜椒粉	Unit 3 Part B
aroma *n.* 香味	Unit 3 Part B
aromatic *adj.* 芳香的,有香味的	Unit 3 Part B
Asia *n.* 亚洲	Unit 3 Part B
assistant *adj.&n.* 助理的;助理	Unit 1 Part A
assistant chef 行政总厨师长助理	Unit 1 Part A
athlete *n.* 运动员,运动选手	Unit 1 Part A
avocado *n.* 鳄梨	Unit 5 Part A

B

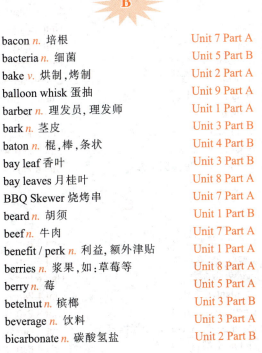

bacon *n.* 培根	Unit 7 Part A
bacteria *n.* 细菌	Unit 5 Part B
bake *v.* 烘制,烤制	Unit 2 Part A
balloon whisk 蛋抽	Unit 9 Part A
barber *n.* 理发员,理发师	Unit 1 Part A
bark *n.* 茎皮	Unit 3 Part B
baton *n.* 棍,棒,条状	Unit 4 Part B
bay leaf 香叶	Unit 3 Part B
bay leaves 月桂叶	Unit 8 Part A
BBQ Skewer 烧烤串	Unit 7 Part A
beard *n.* 胡须	Unit 1 Part B
beef *n.* 牛肉	Unit 7 Part A
benefit / perk *n.* 利益,额外津贴	Unit 1 Part A
berries *n.* 浆果,如:草莓等	Unit 8 Part A
berry *n.* 莓	Unit 5 Part A
betelnut *n.* 槟榔	Unit 3 Part B
beverage *n.* 饮料	Unit 3 Part B
bicarbonate *n.* 碳酸氢盐	Unit 2 Part B

Bird's Nest Soup 燕窝汤	Unit 8 Part B
blade *n.* 肩胛骨	Unit 6 Part A
blender *n.* 绞碎机	Unit 2 Part A
blueberry *n.* 越莓,蓝莓	Unit 5 Part A
boil *n.&v.* 沸点;沸腾;煮沸	Unit 1 Part B
boning knife 去骨刀	Unit 2 Part B
bonus *n.* 奖金,红利	Unit 1 Part A
boring *adj.* 令人厌烦的	Unit 1 Part A
Borsch Moscow Style 莫斯科红菜汤	Unit 8 Part B
braise *v.* 焖	Unit 6 Part A
brandy *n.* 白兰地	Unit 3 Part B
brisket *n.* 胸肉	Unit 6 Part A
broccoli *n.* 花椰菜,花茎甘蓝	Unit 6 Part A
brochette *n.* 烤肉	Unit 6 Part A
broiler *n.* 烤炉	Unit 2 Part A
bruising *n.* 硬伤	Unit 4 Part A
brush *n.* 刷子	Unit 4 Part B
bun *n.* 小圆包	Unit 9 Part A
bun tin/Muffin pan 松饼烤盘	Unit 2 Part B
burner *n.* 火炉;烧火的人	Unit 1 Part B
butcher *n.&v.* 屠夫;屠宰	Unit 1 Part A
butter *n.* 黄油	Unit 7 Part A

C

Caesar Salad 凯撒沙拉	Unit 8 Part B
cake tin/pan 蛋糕烤盘	Unit 2 Part B
calcium *n.* 钙	Unit 4 Part A
calorie *n.* 卡路里(热量单位)	Unit 4 Part A
canapé *n.* 鸡尾小吃	Unit 7 Part A
carbohydrate *n.* 碳水化合物	Unit 4 Part A
career ladder 职务级别提升,(职务)提级	
	Unit 1 Part A
carving knife 雕刻刀	Unit 2 Part B
carving set 一套切肉用具	Unit 2 Part B
casserole 炖锅	Unit 2 Part B
category *n.* 种类,类	Unit 3 Part A
celery *n.* 芹菜	Unit 6 Part B
challenging *adj.* 引起挑战性兴趣的,挑逗的	
	Unit 1 Part A

champagne n. 香槟酒	Unit 3 Part B	cream asparagus soup 芦笋奶油汤	Unit 7 Part B
characteristic adj. 典型的	Unit 4 Part A	cream soup 奶油汤	Unit 7 Part B
cheese knife 切奶酪刀	Unit 2 Part B	crispness n. 脆	Unit 4 Part A
chef n. 厨师长	Unit 1 Part A	croissant n. 牛角包	Unit 9 Part A
chicken n. 鸡	Unit 7 Part A	crunchy adj. 脆的	Unit 6 Part B
Chicken Kiev 黄油鸡卷	Unit 8 Part B	cubed adj.（正方）块状的	Unit 6 Part A
chicken liver pate 鸡肝酱	Unit 7 Part A	cucumber n. 黄瓜	Unit 3 Part A
chief adj. 主要的	Unit 3 Part B	culinary adj. 烹饪的	Unit 3 Part B
chili paste 辣酱	Unit 3 Part B	cupboard n. 橱柜	Unit 2 Part A
chili pepper 红辣椒	Unit 3 Part A	curry powder 咖喱	Unit 3 Part A
chop v. 切细，剁碎	Unit 4 Part B	cutlet n. 肉排，肉片	Unit 6 Part A
n. 一块（肉、排骨）	Unit 6 Part A	cutlet bat 肉片、鱼片球板	Unit 2 Part B
chopper n. 屠刀，大砍刀	Unit 2 Part B		
chopping board 切菜板	Unit 5 Part B	**D**	
chopstick n. 筷子	Unit 7 Part A		
chronic adj. 慢性的，长期的	Unit 5 Part A	dairy n. 乳制品	Unit 10 Part B
chuck n. 牛颈部至肩部的肉	Unit 6 Part A	damp adj. 湿润的	Unit 9 Part B
chunk n.（厚）块	Unit 6 Part A	dark green 深绿色	Unit 4 Part A
chutney n. 酸辣调味品	Unit 3 Part A	decay n. 腐烂	Unit 4 Part A
cinnamon n. 桂皮	Unit 3 Part B	deep frier/fryer 油炸锅，深炸（油）锅	Unit 2 Part A
classic n.&adj. 经典的	Unit 9 Part B	deep fry 炸	Unit 8 Part A
clear soup ("consommé" in French) 清汤		deliver v. 递送，释放	Unit 1 Part A
	Unit 7 Part B	demonstrate v. 示范，展示	Unit 4 Part B
cleaver n. 切肉的大菜刀	Unit 2 Part B	deterioration n. 恶化	Unit 4 Part A
cloves n. 丁香	Unit 3 Part B	diarrhoea n. 腹泻	Unit 5 Part B
cloves of garlic 三瓣蒜	Unit 6 Part A	dice v. 将（菜）切成小块或丁	Unit 4 Part A
coarse adj. 粗的，粗糙的	Unit 3 Part A	dice n. 小方块	Unit 3 Part A
cockroach n. 蟑螂	Unit 10 Part A	diet n. 饮食	Unit 4 Part A
cocktail n. 鸡尾酒	Unit 7 Part A	dishwasher n. 洗碗机	Unit 2 Part A
coffee pot 咖啡壶	Unit 7 Part A	disposal n. 处理，处置	Unit 2 Part A
cold fruit soup 水果冷汤	Unit 7 Part B	doctor n. 医生；博士	Unit 1 Part A
commis n. 实习侍者，助理厨师	Unit 1 Part A	donut n. 多纳圈	Unit 9 Part A
compress v. 挤压	Unit 6 Part B	dough n. 面团	Unit 8 Part B
condiment n. 调味品	Unit 3 Part B	drain n. 排水管	Unit 2 Part A
consommé German 德式清汤	Unit 7 Part B	drainage n. 排水系统；污水	Unit 2 Part A
consume v. 消耗	Unit 5 Part A	dressing n. 加味品	Unit 3 Part A
consumption n. 消费，使用	Unit 3 Part A	drumstick n. 家禽腿下部	Unit 6 Part B
container n. 容器(箱、盆、罐、壶、桶、坛子)			
	Unit 1 Part B	**E**	
cook n. 厨师	Unit 1 Part A		
cooker n. 炊具，蒸(煮)机	Unit 1 Part B	edible adj. 可以吃的	Unit 3 Part A
cooling tray/rack 降温盘	Unit 2 Part B	egg boiler 煮蛋器	Unit 2 Part A
cornmeal n.（粗磨）玉米粉	Unit 6 Part B	egg wash 蛋汁	Unit 6 Part B
cough n. 咳嗽	Unit 1 Part B	eggplant n. 茄子	Unit 4 Part A
counter n. 操作台	Unit 2 Part A	elastic adj. 有弹性的	Unit 8 Part B
cramp n. 绞痛	Unit 10 Part A	electric hand mixer 电动搅拌器	Unit 9 Part A
cream n. 奶油	Unit 8 Part A	end n. 末端，梢，尖	Unit 4 Part B

Vocabulary

equipment *n.* 装备,设备,器材	Unit 1 Part B
Europe *n.* 欧洲	Unit 3 Part B
excessive *adj.* 过多的	Unit 10 Part B
executive *adj.&n.* 执行的;执行者	Unit 1 Part A
executive chef 行政总厨师长	Unit 1 Part A

facility *n.* 设施,设备	Unit 1 Part B
ferment *v.* 使发酵	Unit 5 Part A
fermented *adj.* 发酵的	Unit 3 Part A
fiber *n.* 纤维	Unit 4 Part A
fiery *adj.* 火热的,火辣的	Unit 3 Part B
fillet *n.* 肉片,鱼片	Unit 6 Part A
fine *adv.* 精巧地	Unit 4 Part B
fish *n.* 鱼	Unit 7 Part A
fish scissors 鱼剪刀	Unit 2 Part B
flammable *adj.* 易燃的	Unit 2 Part B
flank *n.* 牛肋腹肉	Unit 6 Part A
flavor *n.* 味道	Unit 5 Part A
flexi-time *n.* 弹性上班制	Unit 1 Part A
flour *n.* 面粉	Unit 8 Part A
foil *n.* 锡纸	Unit 9 Part B
folate *n.* 叶酸	Unit 5 Part A
food processor 加工器	Unit 2 Part A
fork *n.* 叉子	Unit 7 Part A
French onion soup 法式洋葱汤	Unit 7 Part B
fresh *adj.* 新鲜的	Unit 3 Part B
fresh milk 鲜奶	Unit 8 Part A
Fried Pork Chop Milanese 米兰煎猪排	Unit 8 Part B
fry top/grill 烤架	Unit 2 Part A
frying basket 油炸篮(筐),沥油网篮	Unit 2 Part A
frying pan 有柄煎锅	Unit 2 Part B
fungi *n.* 真菌	Unit 10 Part A

garbage *n.* 垃圾,废物	Unit 1 Part B
gardener *n.* 园丁	Unit 1 Part A
garnish (with) *v.* 给……配上	Unit 2 Part B
gastrointestinal *adj.* 肠胃的	Unit 10 Part A
gateau *n.* 奶油蛋糕	Unit 9 Part B
giblet *n.* 内脏	Unit 6 Part B
gin *n.* 金酒	Unit 3 Part B
ginger *n.* 姜	Unit 3 Part A
glyceriner *n.* 甘油	Unit 9 Part B
Goose Liver Pie 鹅肝派	Unit 8 Part B

gradient *n.* 梯度	Unit 6 Part A
grapefruit knife 西柚刀	Unit 2 Part B
grated cheese 奶酪粉	Unit 8 Part A
gravy *n.* 肉汤	Unit 6 Part B
grease *n.* 油脂	Unit 2 Part A
greaseproof paper 防油纸	Unit 9 Part A
green pea puree soup 青豆茸汤	Unit 7 Part B
grill *n.&v.* 铁算子;烤炙室;烤炙	Unit 1 Part A
grill *n.* 炙烤架	Unit 2 Part A
grill *v.* 烤	Unit 6 Part A
grill cook 负责在烤架上烤炙肉类的厨师	Unit 1 Part A
grind *v.* 磨(碾)碎	Unit 4 Part A
ground *adj.* (grind 的过去分词)磨碎的	Unit 3 Part B

hairnet *n.* 发网	Unit 1 Part B
handkerchief *n.* 手帕,纸巾	Unit 1 Part B
handle *v.* 处理	Unit 5 Part B
hardy *adj.* 坚硬的	Unit 4 Part A
Hawaii Seafood Salad 夏威夷海鲜沙拉	Unit 8 Part B
hazardous *adj.* 危险的	Unit 10 Part A
honey *n.* 蜂蜜	Unit 3 Part A
honeydew melon 哈密瓜	Unit 5 Part B
hors-d'oeuvre *n.* 餐前小吃	Unit 7 Part B
horse-radish *n.* 辣根	Unit 3 Part A
hose *v.* 用水管冲洗	Unit 2 Part A
hot *adj.* 辣的	Unit 3 Part A
Hot Pot 火锅	Unit 8 Part B
Huangshan Braised Pigeon 黄山炖鸽	Unit 8 Part B
Hungary *n.* 匈牙利	Unit 3 Part B
hygiene *n.* 卫生	Unit 10 Part A

iced soup 冷汤	Unit 7 Part B
include *v.* 包括,包含	Unit 1 Part B
India *n.* 印度	Unit 3 Part B
indispensable *adj.* 不可缺少的	Unit 2 Part A
Indonesia *n.* 印度尼西亚	Unit 3 Part B
infection *n.* 感染	Unit 10 Part A
ingredient *n.* 成分	Unit 3 Part A
instant *adj.* 立即的,直接的	Unit 5 Part A

investment *n.* 投资，投入	Unit 4 Part A

J

jam *n.* 果酱	Unit 3 Part A
jelly *n.* 果子冻，肉冻	Unit 3 Part A

K

ketchup *n.* 番茄酱	Unit 3 Part A
Kewpie mayonnaise 千岛酱	Unit 7 Part A
kitchen *n.* 厨房	Unit 1 Part A
kitchen cutters 厨房刀具	Unit 2 Part B
kiwi *n.* 猕猴桃	Unit 5 Part A

L

larder *n.* 食品室，餐具室	Unit 1 Part A
larder chef 负责烹饪各种肉类的厨师长	Unit 1 Part A
lather *n.&v.* 肥皂泡；涂以肥皂泡	Unit 1 Part B
lemon *n.* 柠檬	Unit 5 Part A
lemon juice 柠檬汁	Unit 7 Part A
license *n.* 执照，许可证，特许	Unit 1 Part B
lichee *n.* 荔枝	Unit 5 Part A
light yellow 浅黄色	Unit 4 Part A
loaf tin/pan 面包斗	Unit 2 Part B
lobster bisque 龙虾浓汤	Unit 7 Part B
loin *n.* 腰肉	Unit 6 Part A
London Broil 伦敦杂肉扒	Unit 8 Part B

M

macaroni *n.* 通心粉	Unit 8 Part A
madeira *n.* （玛德拉岛产）白葡萄酒	Unit 3 Part B
Madeira cake 马德拉蛋糕	Unit 9 Part B
mainly *adv.* 主要地	Unit 3 Part B
major *adj.* 主要的	Unit 3 Part A
mallard *n.* 野鸭	Unit 6 Part B
mallet *n.* 木槌	Unit 2 Part B
Mandarin Fish 鳜鱼	Unit 8 Part B
maple syrup 枫叶糖浆，汁	Unit 3 Part A
marinate *v.* 浸泡	Unit 6 Part A
marmalade *n.* 橘子酱	Unit 3 Part A

measuring cup 量杯	Unit 7 Part A
mechanic *n.* 技工，机修工	Unit 1 Part A
microorganism *n.* 微生物	Unit 10 Part A
microwave *n.* 微波炉	Unit 2 Part A
mild *adj.* 味淡的	Unit 3 Part B
minced garlic 蒜蓉	Unit 8 Part A
mincer/grinder *n.* 绞肉机	Unit 2 Part A
mineral *n.* 矿物	Unit 5 Part A
mixed BBQ skewer 什锦烧烤串	Unit 7 Part A
mixer *n.* 搅拌器	Unit 2 Part A
mixing bowl 调拌钵	Unit 2 Part B
moisture *n.* 水分	Unit 6 Part B
mop *v.* 用拖把拖洗，擦	Unit 1 Part B
muffin *n.* 马粉包	Unit 9 Part A
mushroom *n.* 蘑菇	Unit 7 Part A
mussel *n.* 贻贝	Unit 6 Part B
mustard *n.* 芥末	Unit 3 Part A

N

nausea *v.* 恶心	Unit 10 Part A
nip *v.* 掐	Unit 6 Part B
North Pole calm 北极贝	Unit 7 Part A
nutmeg *n.* 肉豆蔻	Unit 3 Part B
nutrition *n.* 营养	Unit 4 Part A
nutritious *adj.* 有营养的	Unit 5 Part A
nutty *adj.* 有坚果味的	Unit 3 Part B

O

olive oil 橄榄油	Unit 7 Part A
onion *n.* 洋葱	Unit 3 Part A
onion chopped 碎洋葱	Unit 8 Part A
oregano *n.* 牛至	Unit 3 Part B
organic *adj.* 有机的	Unit 10 Part B
originate *v.* 发源	Unit 3 Part B
oven *n.* 烤箱	Unit 2 Part A
oyster *n.* 牡蛎	Unit 6 Part B
oyster knife 开牡蛎刀	Unit 2 Part B

P

pallet knife 铲刀	Unit 2 Part B
pan fry 煎	Unit 8 Part A
pancake *n.* 薄煎饼	Unit 3 Part A

Vocabulary

panforte *n.* 意大利果包	Unit 9 Part B	puree soup 茸汤	Unit 7 Part B
pantryman *n.* 配膳员，食品管理者	Unit 1 Part A	purple *adj.* 紫色的	Unit 4 Part A
papaya *n.* 木瓜	Unit 5 Part A		
paring knife 水果刀	Unit 2 Part B		
parsley *n.* 欧芹	Unit 6 Part B	**Q**	
pastry *n.* 面点	Unit 1 Part A		
pathogenic *adj.* 病原的	Unit 10 Part A	quick-mix 半成品	Unit 9 Part A
peanut *n.* 花生	Unit 7 Part A		
peel *v.* 削皮	Unit 7 Part B	**R**	
peeling *n.* 剥皮；剥下的皮	Unit 1 Part B		
pension *n.* 养老金，退休金	Unit 1 Part A	radiation *n.* 放射	Unit 10 Part B
Peppery and Hot Chicken 麻辣鸡	Unit 8 Part B	raw *adj.* 生的，未煮熟的	Unit 5 Part B
per your taste 按照您的口味	Unit 6 Part A	recipe *n.* 菜谱	Unit 8 Part B
pie dish 馅饼盘	Unit 2 Part B	red wine 红葡萄酒	Unit 3 Part B
pierce *v.* 刺穿	Unit 6 Part B	refrigerator *n.* 冰箱	Unit 2 Part A
pineapple *n.* 菠萝	Unit 7 Part A	relief *n.* 换班者，接班者	Unit 1 Part A
pint *n.* （量词）品脱	Unit 6 Part A	relish *n.* 酸果，泡菜	Unit 7 Part B
piping nozzle 挤嘴	Unit 9 Part B	remove *v.* 移开，拿开	Unit 1 Part B
pizza *n.* 比萨	Unit 8 Part B	repetitive *adj.* 重复的，反复性的	Unit 1 Part A
places of production 产地	Unit 3 Part B	reporter *n.* 记者，通讯员	Unit 1 Part A
plait bread 辫包	Unit 9 Part A	rewarding *adj.* 报答的，有益的，值得的	Unit 1 Part A
plate *n.* 侧胸腹肉	Unit 6 Part A	rhizomes *n.* 根茎	Unit 3 Part B
plum *n.* 李子	Unit 5 Part A	rhum *n.* 朗姆酒	Unit 3 Part B
poach *v.* 温煮	Unit 8 Part A	rind *n.* 外皮	Unit 6 Part B
policeman *n.* 警察	Unit 1 Part A	rinse *v.* （用清水）刷，冲洗掉	Unit 1 Part B
pomegranate *n.* 石榴	Unit 5 Part A	roast *n.&v.* 烤肉；烤，煨，烘，焙，炒	Unit 1 Part A
port wine 钵酒	Unit 3 Part B	Roasted Suckling Pig 烤乳猪	Unit 8 Part B
porter *n.* 搬运工人	Unit 1 Part A	rock sugar 冰糖	Unit 3 Part B
pot *n.* 罐，壶	Unit 1 Part B	rodent *n.* 啮齿类动物	Unit 10 Part A
potassium *n.* 钾	Unit 5 Part B	roll *n.* 面包卷，卷饼	Unit 3 Part A
potato masher 土豆捣烂器	Unit 2 Part B	rolling pin 擀面杖	Unit 2 Part B
potman *n.* 擦洗锅的人	Unit 1 Part A	round *n.* 牛腿肉	Unit 6 Part A
poultry *n.* 家禽	Unit 5 Part B	rule *n.* 规则，惯例，章程	Unit 1 Part B
poultry shears 家禽拔毛剪	Unit 2 Part B	rump *n.* 后腿部的牛排	Unit 6 Part A
prawn *n.* 对虾	Unit 7 Part A		
preheat *v.* 预热	Unit 8 Part B	**S**	
preservative *n.* 防腐剂	Unit 3 Part A		
preserve *v.* 保持	Unit 3 Part B	sack *n.* 袋子，大包	Unit 4 Part B
pressure cooker 高压锅	Unit 2 Part B	saffron *n.* 番红花	Unit 3 Part B
prime rib 主肋骨，大肋骨	Unit 6 Part A	salami *n.* 意大利蒜味香肠	Unit 2 Part B
procedure *n.* 程序，手续	Unit 1 Part B	salmon *n.* 三文鱼	Unit 6 Part B
process *n.* 过程	Unit 3 Part A	salt *n.* 盐	Unit 3 Part A
produce *v.* 生产	Unit 3 Part B	salty *adj.* 咸的	Unit 3 Part A
promotion *n.* 提拔，晋升	Unit 1 Part A	sanitation *n.* 公共卫生	Unit 10 Part B
protein *n.* 蛋白质	Unit 4 Part A	sanitation *n.* 卫生设备	Unit 2 Part A
pumpkin *n.* 南瓜	Unit 4 Part B	satisfying *adj.* 令人满足的，令人满意的	Unit 1 Part A
pungent *adj.* 刺鼻的，辣的	Unit 3 Part B		

saturated *adj.* 浸透的；充满的	Unit 6 Part B	sponge *n.* 海绵蛋糕	Unit 9 Part A
saturated fat 饱和脂肪	Unit 9 Part B	spread *v.* 涂抹食品	Unit 3 Part A
sauce *n.* 调味汁，调味料	Unit 1 Part A	spring onion 生吃的小洋葱，葱	Unit 4 Part B
saucepan *n.* 深平底锅	Unit 2 Part B	sprinkle (with) *v.* 把……撒在……上	Unit 2 Part B
sauté *v. & adj.* 煎(的)	Unit 6 Part A	sprite *n.* 烈性酒	Unit 7 Part B
scaler *n.* 去鱼鳞器	Unit 2 Part B	staff *n.* 工作人员(全体)，职员(全体)	Unit 1 Part A
scallion *n.* 大葱	Unit 6 Part A	star fruit 杨桃	Unit 5 Part A
scallop *n.* 扇贝	Unit 6 Part B	steam *v.* 蒸	Unit 8 Part A
scrub *v.* 洗擦，擦净	Unit 1 Part B	steamer *n.* 蒸锅	Unit 2 Part B
sea cucumber 海参	Unit 7 Part A	steel *n.* 磨刀用的工具	Unit 2 Part B
seafood soup 海鲜汤	Unit 7 Part B	stew *v.* 烩	Unit 8 Part A
seasoning *n.* 佐料	Unit 3 Part B	steward *n.* 厨房清扫工人	Unit 1 Part A
seed *adj.* 种子	Unit 3 Part B	stopper *n.* 塞子	Unit 2 Part A
segment *n.* 部分，一小块	Unit 6 Part A	store *v.* 存放	Unit 4 Part A
segregate *v.* 隔离	Unit 10 Part B	stove *n.* 炉	Unit 1 Part B
sew *v.* 缝	Unit 6 Part B	strainer *n.* 滤器，滤网	Unit 2 Part B
shaker *n.* 调味瓶	Unit 3 Part A	strawberry *n.* 草莓	Unit 7 Part B
shank *n.* (牛羊等的)腿	Unit 6 Part A	stressful *adj.* 产生压力的，使紧迫的	Unit 1 Part A
shellfish *n.* 贝	Unit 7 Part A	stuffing *n.* 填充物	Unit 6 Part B
sherry *n.* 雪利酒	Unit 3 Part B	substance *n.* 物质	Unit 5 Part A
shred *v.* 切(丝)	Unit 7 Part B	sugar *n.* 糖	Unit 3 Part A
sieve *n.* 筛子	Unit 2 Part B	supply *n.* 补给，供给，供应品	Unit 1 Part A
simmer *v.* 慢慢地煮	Unit 6 Part A	surrender *v.* 交出；放弃，听任	Unit 1 Part B
sink *n.* 水槽，水池	Unit 1 Part A	sweep *v.* 扫，打扫，清扫	Unit 1 Part B
sirloin *n.* 牛腰肉	Unit 6 Part A	sweet *adj.* 甜的	Unit 3 Part A
skewer/brochette *n.* 串肉扦	Unit 2 Part B	swirl *n.* 旋涡状	Unit 9 Part B
slant *adj.* 斜的	Unit 6 Part A	symptom *v.* 症状	Unit 10 Part A
slaughter *n.* 宰杀	Unit 10 Part B		
slice *n.* 片，薄片	Unit 3 Part A		
slice *v. & n.* 切片，薄片	Unit 6 Part A		
smoked salmon canapés 熏三文鱼鸡尾小吃	Unit 7 Part A		

Snails in Shell Herb Butter 焗蜗牛	Unit 8 Part B	tangerine *n.* 橘子	Unit 5 Part A
sneeze *v.* 打喷嚏	Unit 1 Part A	tea cup 茶杯	Unit 7 Part A
soft drink 软饮料	Unit 7 Part A	tenderloin *n.* 腰部嫩肉	Unit 6 Part A
soup *n.* 汤	Unit 1 Part A	texture *n.* 质地	Unit 6 Part B
sour *adj.* 酸的	Unit 3 Part A	the Philippines 菲律宾	Unit 3 Part B
Sour West Lake Fish 西湖醋鱼	Unit 8 Part A	thick soup (broth) 浓汤	Unit 7 Part B
sous-chef *n.* 〔法〕副厨师长	Unit 1 Part A	tin opener 开罐器	Unit 7 Part A
soy sauce 酱油	Unit 3 Part A	tiramisu *n.* 提拉米苏	Unit 9 Part A
soybean paste 黄酱	Unit 3 Part A	title *n.* 头衔，官衔，职别	Unit 1 Part A
Spaghetti *n.* 意大利面	Unit 8 Part B	toaster *n.* 烤面包机	Unit 2 Part A
spatula *n.* 刮铲，抹刀	Unit 2 Part B	tomato *n.* 番茄	Unit 7 Part A
spice *n.* 香料	Unit 3 Part A	tomato sauce 番茄酱	Unit 3 Part A
spicy *adj.* 香的，辛辣的	Unit 3 Part A	topping *n.* (食品上面的)配品	Unit 3 Part A
spinach *n.* 芹菜	Unit 8 Part A	toxication *n.* 中毒	Unit 10 Part A
split *v.* 切开	Unit 2 Part B	trace *n.* 痕迹	Unit 5 Part A
		trim *v.* 整理，修剪	Unit 2 Part B
		trim off 修剪	Unit 4 Part A

Vocabulary

trout *n.* 鳟鱼	Unit 6 Part B
tsp= table spoon 茶匙	Unit 9 Part B
tub *n.* 水龙头	Unit 2 Part A
tuna *n.* 金枪鱼	Unit 6 Part B
turnip *n.* 萝卜	Unit 5 Part A
turntable *n.* 转台	Unit 9 Part B

utensil *n.* 器具	Unit 1 Part B

valid *adj.* [律]有效的, 正当的	Unit 1 Part B
vegetable *n.* 植物, 蔬菜	Unit 1 Part A
vegetable soup 蔬菜汤	Unit 7 Part B
ventilation *n.* 通风, 流通空气	Unit 1 Part B
versatile *adj.* 通用的, 多方面适用的	Unit 3 Part A
vinegar *n.* 醋	Unit 3 Part A
vomit *v.* 呕吐	Unit 5 Part B

waiter *n.* 男服务员	Unit 1 Part A
Waldorf Salad 华道夫沙拉	Unit 8 Part B
wasabi *n.* 青芥末	Unit 3 Part A
waste bin 废物箱; 垃圾箱	Unit 1 Part B
watermelon *n.* 西瓜	Unit 7 Part A
whisky *n.* 威士忌	Unit 3 Part B
white wine 白葡萄酒	Unit 3 Part B
wine *n.* 葡萄酒	Unit 7 Part B
wipe *v.* 擦, 擦去	Unit 1 Part B
wok *n.* 炒菜锅	Unit 2 Part B
Worcestershire sauce 辣椒油	Unit 3 Part A
wrapper *n.* 包装材料, 包装纸	Unit 1 Part B

Key to Exercises

Unit 1   Kitchen Introduction

Part A
Start You Off

Activity 2

Money	Hours	Benefits/Perks
very well-paid	long hours	a company car
a pretty good salary	do overtime	pension scheme
a regular pay rise	flexi-time	private health insurance
bonus	go part-time	

Promotion	Holiday
get promoted	six week's paid holiday
work your way up	taking a few days off
career ladder	

Focus on Language

1. She is in the college and studying computer science.
2. He's a doctor; he loves his work and thinks it is very rewarding.
3. She's a journalist. She works for BEIJING YOUTH DAILY.

Language Tips

1. Asking about the occupation

   Task 3

TERM	DEFINITION
Relief Cook	The person who can relieve everyone.
Aboyeur	The person who works between cook and guest, and carries orders to the cook.
Breakfast Cook	The person who makes the breakfast.
Butcher	The person who cuts the meat and slaughters the animals.
Potman	The person who washes and scrubs pans and pots.
Roast Cook	The person who puts the meat into the oven.
Pantryman	The person who is responsible for the pantry.

2. Expressing your attitudes toward your job

   Task 1

   1 e   2 c   3 a   4 b   5 d   6 f

Part B
Focus on Language

Listening

Personal Health Cleanliness and Safety in the Kitchen

1. Hands must be <u>thoroughly washed</u> before starting work, after handling food, after <u>smoking</u>, after <u>using</u> the

toilet and after using a handkerchief or tissue. The hand sink in the production area must be used for hand washing. The sink in the restroom must be used after using the restroom facilities. Hands must be washed with hot soapy water for a minimum of 20 seconds and dried with a paper towel.

2. All cuts must be bandaged with waterproof protectors, and watertight disposable gloves should be worn.
3. Kitchen staff with open lesions, infected wounds, sore throats or any communicable diseases shall not be permitted to work in the kitchen.
4. No eating or drinking permitted in the kitchen area. No use of tobacco products allowed in the kitchen.
5. Kitchen staff shall be clean and well groomed. Clothing should be made of a washable fabric. No open-toed shoes are to be worn in the kitchen.
6. All the kitchen staff is to wear hair restraints provided by the kitchen. This includes the use of both hair and beard nets as necessary.
7. Personal belongings must be kept out of food preparation and storage areas. All personal belongings are to be stored in the designated area or off premises.
8. Remove all insecure jewelry that might fall into food or equipment. Remove hand jewelry when manipulating food by hand

Language Tips

1. Asking about the Procedure
Task 1
wet   soap   lather   scrub   rinse   dry

Do Extension Activities

Activity 1
1. clean   2. clear   3. empty   4. put   5. throw out

Activity 2
Yes.   No.   No.   Yes.   Yes.

Unit 2   Kitchen Facilities

Part A
Start You Off
Activity 1

1. Freezer	2. Cold Kitchen	3. Butchery	4. Pastry	5. Beverage Cooler	9. Pick-up Area
6. Kitchen Store	7. Chef's Office				
	10. Pot-washer	8. Hot Kitchen			
		11. Vegetable Preparation	12. Fish Section	13. Scullery	

1. 冷冻箱、冰箱   2. 冷菜制作间
3. 屠宰房   4. 面点间、糕点间
5. 饮料冷却器/间   6. 厨房库房
7. 厨师办公室   8. 通过火加工烹饪菜肴制作间
9. 餐厅与厨房之间的备菜室 10. 厨具洗净器
11. 蔬菜配制间   12. 鱼的制作间

13. 食器洗涤室

Activity 2

A	B
1. executive chef (k)	a. 喊菜的服务员
2. grill cook (h)	b. 厨房唱单员
3. fish cook (g)	c. 屠夫
4. pastry chef (l)	d. 服务员
5. vegetable chef (m)	e. 负责擦洗大深锅的人
6. butcher (c)	f. 厨房清扫工人
7. aboyeur (a)	g. 负责烹饪鱼的厨师
8. commis (j)	h. 负责在烤架上烤灸肉类的厨师
9. kitchen clerk (b)	i. 厨房搬运工
10. pot-man (e)	j. 学徒工
11. kitchen porter (i)	k. 行政总厨师长
12. steward (f)	l. 面点厨师
13. waiter (d)	m. 负责烹饪蔬菜的厨师

Focus on Language

Listening

Areas in the Kitchen	Function of the Areas
Cooking Area	where the final products come out
Preparing and Cutting Area	where the initial processing, including cutting, dish arranging, is done
Auxiliary Area	which includes storage space such as pantry, refrigerator, etc., dish washing area and changing closet.

Language Tips

1. Floor plan

Practice 1

Freezer	Cold Kitchen	Butchery	Pastry	Beverage Cooler	
Kitchen Store/ Pantry Area	Chef's Office	Hot Kitchen			Pick-up Area
	Pot-washer	Vegetable Preparation	Fish Section	Scullery	

1. Where is the executive chef?
   He is in the <u>chef's office</u>.
2. Where is the grill cook?
   He is in the <u>hot kitchen</u>.
3. Where is the fish cook?
   He is in the <u>fish section</u>.
4. Where is the pastry chef?
   He is in the <u>pastry</u>.
5. Where is the vegetable chef?
   He is in the <u>vegetable preparation</u>.
6. Where is the butcher?
   He is in the <u>butchery</u>.
7. Where is the aboyeur?
   He is in the <u>pick-up area</u>.
8. Where is the commis?
   He is in the <u>chef's office</u>.
9. Where is the kitchen clerk?
   He is in the <u>chef's office</u>.

10. Where is the pot-man?

  He is in the pot-washer.

11. Where is the kitchen porter?

  He is in the kitchen store.

12. Where is the steward?

  He is in the scullery.

13. Where is the waiter?

  He is in the beverage cooler.

2. The equipment in the kitchen

Practice 1

1. oven   2. refrigerator   3. cupboard   4. counter   5. shelf   6. electric steamer

Practice 2

1. sink 水槽

2. tub 水龙头

3. drain 排水管

4. stopper（水池的）塞子

5. garbage disposal（水池下的）废物处理机

6. dishwasher 洗碗机

3. The facilities in the cooking area

Practice 1

Picture 1: stove

Picture 2: deep frier/fryer(frying basket)

Picture 3: egg boiler

Picture 4: fry top

Picture 5: mincer

Picture 6: electric mixer

Picture 7: blender

Picture 8: broiler

Picture 9: burner

Give It a Try

Task 1

1. Toaster 烤面包机   Description：

  It is an electrical machine that you put slices of bread in to make toast.

2. Dishwasher 洗碗机   Description：

  It is a machine for washing plates, cups, bowls, etc.

3. Food Processor 食物加工器   Description：

  It is a piece of equipment that is used to mix or cut up food.

4. Microwave 微波炉   Description:

  It is a type of oven that cooks or heats food very quickly using electromagnetic waves rather than heat.

Task 2

  Where should we put the refrigerators in the kitchen? Refrigerators should not be placed(1) either close to cooking area(2), or washing area(3) to prevent power failure due to heat and water(4). The materials used for the equipment(5) in the kitchen should be of water proof(6) because kitchen is a wet and humid place(7). Also materials should not be flammable(易燃的) for fire(8) is indispensable(不可缺少的) in the kitchen.

Do Extension Activities

Activity 1

1. h   2. i   3. j/n   4. k   5. n/j   6. l   7. m

8. g   9. f   10. e   11. d   12. c   13. b   14. a

Activity 2

1. l   2. m   3. j   4. k   5. i   6. h   7. g

8. f   9. e   10. d   11. c   12. b   13. a   14. n

Activity 3
Example Answer:

Storage Areas for Food
▸ Dry storage
▸ Refrigerator-freezer
The Function of the Storage Areas
✽ Dry storage areas are used for foods and various supplies to be kept.
✽ Refrigerator-freezer areas are needed for products that have to be stored at the temperatures of 35° F to 40° F (1.7° C to 4.4° C) and -10° F to -20° F (-23° C to -28.9° C) respectively.
Items Stored in the Dry Storage Areas
◆ Vegetables, fruits, linens, towels, paper goods, glassware, silverware and furniture.
Temperature in the Storeroom
✽ At a temperature range of 50° F to 70° F (10° C to 21° C) in the dry storage areas.

Part B
Tools and Utensils for Food Production
Start You Off

Activity 1
1. mortar (pestle 杵)   2. coffee grinder   3. timer
4. nutcracker   5. ice cream portioner   6. sieve/sifter
7. lemon squeezer/ juicer   8. grater   9. garlic press

Activity 2
1. peeler 削皮刀   2. butter cutlery (黄油刀)   3. melon scoop(崴球勺)
4. apple corer   5. pizza cutter   6. colander
7. whisk/egg beater   8. ladle   9. slotted spoon 带孔的、带口的勺

Activity 3
1. jar opener 开罐器   2. tin/can opener 开罐器
3. bottle opener 开瓶器   4. corkscrew 瓶塞钻

Focus on Language
Language Tips

1. The equipment and utensils for baking, frying roasting, grilling broiling, etc.

Practice 1
1. mixing bowl 调拌钵   2. cake tin/pan 蛋糕烤盘   3. loaf tin/pan 面包斗
4. cooling tray/rack 降温盘   5. pie dish 馅饼盘   6. bun tin/muffin pan 松饼烤盘
7. pastry 油酥面团   8. flour 面粉   9. rolling pin 擀面杖

Practice 2
Cakes: flour, mixing bowl, pastry, cake tin/pan
Muffin: flour, mixing bowl, pastry, bun tin/muffin pan, cooling tray/rack
Bread: flour, mixing bowl, pastry, loaf tin/pan,
Pie: flour, mixing bowl, pastry, rolling pin, pie dish

Key to Exercises

Practice 3

1. frying pan 有柄煎锅   Description:
        Frying pan is used to fry meat, fish, eggs, etc.

2. oven 烤箱   Description:
        Oven is used to roast large pieces of meat, potatoes, etc. by covering the surface of the food with oil.

3. pressure cooker 高压锅   Description:
        Pressure cooker is used to cook food quickly by steam under high pressure.

4. grill 炙烤架   Description:
        Grill is used to grill meat, shrimp, bacon, sausages, etc.

5. wok 炒菜锅   Description:
        Wok is used to stir-fry different dishes, rice, etc.

6. casserole 炖锅   Description:
        Casserole is used to cook meat, hot dishes, etc. in liquid.

7. saucepan 深平底锅   Description:
        Saucepan is used to boil vegetables, eggs, rice, etc.

8. steamer 蒸锅   Description:
        Steamer is used to steam fish, vegetables, etc. by placing the food above boiling water in a container with holes so that the steam reaches it and covers it.

2. Different tools for preparing meat, fish, vegetables, fruits, etc.
   Practice
   Example:

   A. What do you call this?
   B. It's a <u>whisk</u>.
   A. What are you going to do with it?
   B. I'm going to <u>beat eggs</u> with it.

1. potato masher 土豆捣烂器
   A. What do you call this?   B. It's a <u>potato masher</u>.
   A. What are you going to do with it?   B. I'm going to <u>mash potatoes</u> with it.

2. sieve 筛子
   A. What do you call this?   B. It's a <u>sieve</u>.
   A. What are you going to do with it?   B. I'm going to <u>to sift(v.筛) flour, breadcrumbs or icing sugar</u> with it.

3. cutlet bat 肉片、鱼片球板
   A. What do you call this?   B. It's a <u>cutlet bat</u>.
   A. What are you going to do with it?   B. I'm going to <u>flatten meat</u> with it.

4. skewer/brochette 串肉扦
   A. What do you call this?   B. It's a <u>skewer/brochette</u>.
   A. What are you going to do with it?   B. I'm going to <u>make shish kebabs</u> (羊肉串)with it.

5. mallet 木槌
   A. What do you call this?   B. It's a <u>mallet</u>.
   A. What are you going to do with it?   B. I'm going to <u>beat the meat</u> with it.

6. steel 磨刀用的工具
   A. What do you call this?   B. It's a <u>steel</u>.
   A. What are you going to do with it?   B. I'm going to <u>sharpen the knife</u> with it.

7. wooden spoon 木铲
   A. What do you call this?   B. It's a <u>wooden spoon</u>.
   A. What are you going to do with it?   B. I'm going to <u>stir the ingredients in the bowl/pan</u> with it.

8. scaler 去鱼鳞器
   A. What do you call this?
   B. It's a scaler.
   A. What are you going to do with it?
   B. I'm going to scale the fish with it.

3. Different knives and scissors for preparing meat, fish, vegetables, fruits, etc.
   Practice
   Example:

   A. What do you call this?
   B. It's a whisk.
   A. What are you going to do with it?
   B. I'm going to beat eggs with it.

1. pallet knife 铲刀
   A. What do you call this?
   B. It's a pallet knife.
   A. What are you going to do with it?
   B. I'm going to put chocolate icing on the cake with it.

2. paring knife 水果刀
   A. What do you call this?
   B. It's a paring knife.
   A. What are you going to do with it?
   B. I'm going to peel fruits with it.

3. grapefruit knife 西柚刀
   A. What do you call this?
   B. It's a grapefruit knife.
   A. What are you going to do with it?
   B. I'm going to cut the grapefruit with it.

4. fish scissors 鱼剪刀
   A. What do you call this?
   B. It's a pair of fish scissors.
   A. What are you going to do with it?
   B. I'm going to gut (v.取出肚肠) the fish with it.

5. poultry shears 家禽拔毛剪
   A. What do you call this?
   B. It's a pair of poultry shears.
   A. What are you going to do with it?
   B. I'm going to cut up chicken with it.

6. kitchen cutters 厨房刀具
   A. What do you call this?
   B. It's a pair of kitchen cutters.
   A. What are you going to do with it?
   B. I'm going to cut things with it.

7. cleaver 切肉的大菜刀
   A. What do you call this?
   B. It's a cleaver.
   A. What are you going to do with it?
   B. I'm going to chop up the beef with it.

8. chopper 屠刀、大砍刀
   A. What do you call this?
   B. It's a chopper.
   A. What are you going to do with it?
   B. I'm going to chop some lamb with it.

9. oyster knife 开牡蛎刀
   A. What do you call this?
   B. It's an oyster knife.
   A. What are you going to do with it?
   B. I'm going to open oyster shells with it.

10. boning knife 去骨刀
    A. What do you call this?
    B. It's a boning knife.
    A. What are you going to do with it?
    B. I'm going to remove bones from meat with it.

Give It a Try
Task 1
Example Answers:
Conversation 1
The Vegetable Chef is asking the Commis Cook to:

Key to Exercises

★ wash the spring onions.
★ Trim (vt. 整理、修剪)off both ends.
★ Split(vt. 切开) the spring onions down the middle.

Conversation 2

The Vegetable Chef is asking the Commis Cook to:

★ peel the garlic.
★ crush the garlic and then grind it.
★ add the salt to the garlic.
★ mix the garlic with butter.

Conversation 3

The Vegetable Chef is asking the Commis Cook to:

★ wash the cucumbers.
★ peel the cucumbers.
★ slice the cucumbers up.

Conversation 4

The Vegetable Chef is asking the Commis Cook to:

★ wash the cauliflower well.
★ soak the cauliflower in salt water for thirty minutes.
★ boil the cauliflower in water with lemon juice to keep it white.

Task 2

1. d, c, b, a   2. c, e, a, d, b   3. b, e, c, a, d   4. e, a, d, c, b

Task 3

The Names of Different Knives	The Functions of the Knives
Boning knife	It is used to remove bones from meat./It's for removing bones from meat.
Oyster knife	It is used to open oyster shells./It's for opening oyster shells.
Carving knife	It is used to carve the roast./It is used for carving the roast.
Cheese knife	It is used to cut cheese./It is used for cutting cheese.

Task 4

Model:

Commis: What do you call this tray?
Chef: It's a roasting tray.
Commis: What are you going to do with it?
Chef: I'm going to heat oil in it.
Commis: And then?
Chef: We'll roast chicken.
Commis: I see. And what shall I do?
Chef: Put the roasting tray in the oven.

Situations:

a. To fry potatoes in a sauté pan.

Example answer:

Commis: What do you call this pan?
Chef: It's a sauté pan.
Commis: What are you going to do?
Chef: I'm going to melt butter.
Commis: Why?

Chef:　　　　I will fry potatoes in the pan.
Commis:　　　I see.

b. To make a stew.

Example answer:
Commis:　　　What do you need?
Chef:　　　　I want a stew pan.
Commis:　　　Here you are. Are we going to make a stew?
Chef:　　　　That's right.
Commis:　　　How to cook the stew over a low fire?
Chef:　　　　Yes. We'll simmer the stew.

c. To mince or grind meat.

Example answer:
Commis:　　　What is this?
Chef:　　　　You can call it a mincer or a grinder.
Commis:　　　What is it used for?
Chef:　　　　It minces or grinds meat.
Commis:　　　Can you show me how to use it?
Chef:　　　　Of course.

d. To use a machine to slice things.

Example answer:
Commis:　　　What is this machine called in English?
Chef:　　　　It's an electric slicer.
Commis:　　　What do you slice on it?
Chef:　　　　You can slice ham and salami.(n.意大利蒜味香肠)
Commis:　　　Only ham and salami?
Chef:　　　　Not really. You can slice many other things.
Commis:　　　I see.

Do Extension Activities

Activity 2

1. How do you make French fries?（炸薯条）
   Description:
   　　　Put the potato chips in a frying basket. And then put the frying basket in the deep frier/fryer.
2. How do you make mayonnaise?（蛋黄酱）
   Description:
   　　　Put the eggs in a bowl and add some vinegar, salt, lemon juice and oil. Beat the ingredients with a whisk. You will soon have mayonnaise.
3. How do you roast meat?（盘烤肉）
   Description:
   　　　Heat oil in a roasting tray and put the meat in it. Then put the roasting tray in the oven to roast it.
4. How do you braise beef?（炖牛肉）
   Description:
   　　　Sear(v. 烙黄、烤焦) the beef in hot fat. Then put it in a braising pan and cook it very showly.

Key to Exercises

Unit 3 Condiments

Part A
Start You Off
Activity 1

mustard   salt   vinegar   curry   Worcestershire sauce   sugar

Activity 2

tomato paste   syrup   soy sauce   chili paste   wasabi   salt & pepper

Focus on Language
1. T   2. F   3. F   4. T

Language Tips
1. **Classifying condiments**

   Practice 1
   1. Salt.
   2. People put it on the table as condiment and also use it as ingredient in many other condiments and on a wide range of foods, including vegetables, meats, fish, and poultry.
   3. Salt is a major preservative and is commonly found in most processed foods today.

   Practice 2
   1. the most common condiments
   2. honey or maple syrup
   3. directly in everything from bitter beverages such as tea, to a topping for breakfast cereals
   4. in making other condiments such as jams, jellies, marmalades and are used on bread, rolls and in pastries
   5. on pancakes

2. **Talking about the flavor of condiments**

   Practice 1

咖喱粉	盐	辣椒油	糖	青芥末
curry	salt	Worcestershire sauce	sugar	wasabi
spicy	salty	hot and spicy	sweet	hot and spicy

   Practice 2

   1. spicy and hot   a. 辣
   2. sour   b. 酸
   3. sweet   c. 甜
   4. bitter   d. 苦
   5. salty   e. 咸

   Practice 3

honey	蜂蜜	sweet
garlic	大蒜	hot and spicy
maple syrup	枫叶糖浆 / 汁	sweet
chili pepper	红辣椒	hot and spicy
ginger	姜	hot and spicy
soybean paste	黄酱	salty
rock sugar	冰糖	sweet

Give It a Try

Task 1
1. Pickled condiments date back to the ancient world in Europe as well as Asia.
2. Common pickled foods used as condiments today include ginger, chutney and cucumbers.
3. They are served whole, in slices, or diced.

Task 2
fourth   spicy   black   chili   garlic   onions   Asia   served   western   usually   before

Do Extension Activities

Activity 1
1. ketchup   Worcestershire sauce   fish sauces   soy sauce
   salad dressings   curries   barbecue sauces
2. ancient Mediterranean, Southeast Asia

Activity 2
- Smooth and Lasting   • Served as spread or dressing
- Hot but sweet   • No preservatives

Activity 3
盐 salt   糖 sugar   香油 sesame oil   蚝油 oyster oil
酱油 soy sauce   醋 vinegar   番茄酱 tomato paste   辣酱 chili sauce
胡椒 pepper   桂皮 cinnamon   蜂蜜 honey   咖喱 curry
芥末 mustard   味精 gourmet powder

Activity 4
1. 5, vinegar, tomato, curry, mustard
2. 8, herb, wine, apple, white

Part B

Start You Off

Activity 1

spices

bay leaf

pepper

Activity 2

thyme

nutmeg

betelnut

cinnamon

saffron

cloves

Key to Exercises

Focus on Language
parts plants root bark leaf flower fruit seed

Language Tips
1. Discussing the culinary uses of spices
   Practice 1
   1. Bay leaf is a kind of spice and widely used throughout the world.
   2. It may be best used in soups, sauces, stews and it is an appropriate seasoning for fish, meat and poultry.
   3. It is often included as a pickling spice.
   Practice 2
   1. 3 kinds of peppers are mentioned. They are white, black and green peppers.
   2. It is best ground directly onto food. With hot food it is best to add pepper well towards the end of the cooking process, to preserve its aroma.
   3. Because black pepper would give the sauce a speckled appearance.
   4. Green peppercorns can be mashed with garlic, cinnamon or to make a spiced butter or with cream to make a fresh and attractive sauce for fish.

2. Talking about the flavor of spices
   Practice 1
   Nutmeg is nutty and slightly sweet.
   Cloves are sweetly pungent and strongly aromatic.
   Cinnamon is warm and aromatic.
   Practice 2
   1. F   2. F   3. T

Give It a Try
   Task 1
   more, cakes, baked, puddings, fruit, apples, pears, Middle Eastern, North African, lamb

Do Extension Activities
   Activity 1

Meat	Vegetables	
veal	tomatoes	asparagus
lamb	onions	green beans
beef	cucumbers	broccoli
poultry	carrots	sweet peppers
fish	eggplant	potatoes
	leeks	spinach
	mushrooms	peas

Listen to the tape again and speak out what else work well with thyme.
sausages soups bread herbed butters herbed mayonnaise mustard corn cheese eggs rice

   Activity 2
   aprika   slightly sweet   Hungary
   oregano   bitter and strongly aromatic   Europe, West and South Asia
   betelnut   slightly bitter & strongly aromatic   Indonesia, the Philippines, India

   Activity 3
   leaves or branches of aromatic plants

ripened fruits or seeds of plants
roots or bulbs of certain plants

Activity 4

I. 1. T   2. F   3. T   4. T   5. T   6. F

II. 1. In cooked recipes, Basil is generally added at the last moment, because cooking quickly destroys the flavor.

2. Basil can be kept for a short time in plastic bags in the refrigerator, or for a longer period in the freezer, after being blanched quickly in boiling water.

3. Hyssop leaves should be used sparingly because the flavor is very strong.

4. It is often used dried and in cooking Iranian, Arabic, Central Asian, European, Indian and Turkish cuisines as a seasoning and coloring.

5. Chives are the smallest species of the onion family.

6. In cooking different kinds of meat.

7. Hyssop leaf and Saffron.

III.
A	B
chives	widely used as condiments for fish, pancakes, potatoes and soups.
fennel leaves	often used in egg, fish and other dishes
sage	often used in cooking meat and vegetable soups
saffron	contributing a yellow-orange coloring to foods

Unit 4   Food Material I

Part A
Start You Off

Activity 1

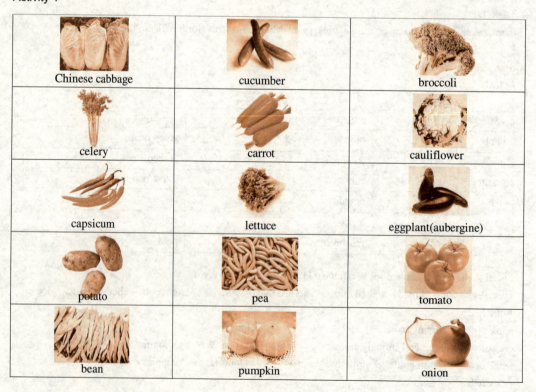

Key to Exercises

Activity 2

图 1 红色 red	图 2 蓝色 blue	图 3 黄色 yellow	图 4 黑色 black
图 5 绿色 green	图 6 白色 white	图 7 紫色 purple	图 8 棕色 brown
图 9 深绿色 dark green	图 10 浅黄色 light yellow	图 11 灰色 grey	图 12 橙色 orange

Focus on language

How to Choose Vegetables
LANGUAGE TIPS
Practice 1

Fresh vegetables	Bad vegetables
freshness; bright, lively color and crispness; best quality;	injury, bruising, damage, decay, deterioration

Practice 2

1. When you buy vegetables, the most important thing you need to consider is <u>freshness</u>.
2. The characteristic signs of freshness are <u>bright, lively color and crispness</u>.
3. Vegetables are usually at their <u>best quality and price</u> at the peak of their season.
4. You should be very careful to <u>prevent injury</u> to vegetables.
5. The consumer pays for <u>carelessness</u> in the long run.
6. It isn't a good idea to buy vegetables of <u>low price alone</u>.
7. Don't buy <u>more</u> vegetables than you can properly store in your refrigerator.
8. <u>Root</u> vegetables can be stored for more than one week.
9. It's a waste of money to buy fresh vegetables <u>affected by decay</u>.
10. Even if you cut off the decayed area, <u>rapid deterioration</u> is likely to spread to other areas.

Practice 3

1. Freshness is important.
2. Check the characteristic signs of freshness such as bright, lively color and crispness.
3. At the peak of their season.
4. Carefulness.
5. No, because you can not store them very long.
6. Most vegetables can be stored for 2 to 5 days, except for root vegetables, which can be stored from 1 to several weeks.
7. Decay. Because even if you do trim off the decayed area, rapid deterioration is likely to spread to other areas.

Give it a try

Task 1

1. eggplant   2. Tomatoes

3. Cabbage   4. Leek
5. Carrots   6. cauliflower
7. Capsicums 8. pumpkins
9. celery   10. Cucumbers

Task 2
1. demand   2. prevent   3. check   4. avoided
5. because of 6. are likely to

Do Extension Activities

Activity 1
1. easy   2. plain   3. hard   4. fit   5. main   6. thin

Activity 2

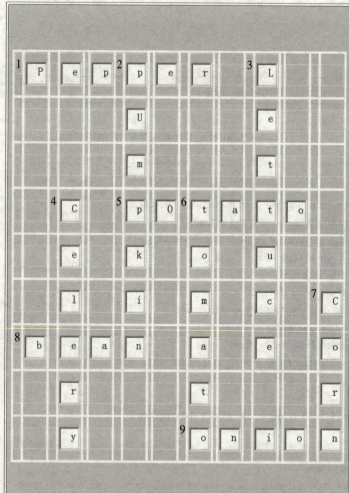

Across

1. Some are used to make hot sauce. Some aren't hot at all.
5. You can bake, mash or fry it.
8. Soy ___ is widely cultivated for its nutritious seeds.
9. You often cry when you cut it.

Down

2. You make a Jack-o'-Lantern with this vegetable.
3. It's a green leaf used in salads and hamburgers.
4. It's a high-fiber, stringy stalk, used in soups or salads.
6. You cook it to prepare red sauce.
7. Many people eat ___ flakes for breakfast.

Key to Exercises

Part B
Start You Off
Activity 1

beat　　　　grate　　　　squeeze　　　slice　　　　chop　　　　peel

Activity 2

1. g 2. h 3. f 4. j 5. i 6. a 7. c 8. e 9. d 10. b

Focus on Language
Language Tips
1. **Ways of preparing vegetables**
   Practice 2
   3　4　1　2
   Practice 3
   1. What <u>shall</u> I do?
   2. You wash these <u>cucumbers</u>.
   3. And peel <u>them</u>.
   4. <u>Slice</u> the cucumbers up.
   5. We shall <u>make</u> the cucumber salad.
   6. Shall I <u>wash</u> the cauliflower?
   7. You wash it <u>well</u>.
   8. Cauliflower is <u>always</u> dirty.
   9. <u>Soak</u> the cauliflower in salt water.
   10. For how <u>many</u> minutes?
   11. Split the cauliflower into <u>small pieces</u>.
   12. How <u>shall</u> I cook the cauliflower?
   13. You <u>boil</u> it in water <u>with</u> lemon juice.
   14. The lemon juice will <u>keep</u> it white.

Give it a try
Task 1
1. <u>Remove</u> the seeds.
2. <u>Stuff/Wash</u> the peppers.
3. <u>Slice</u> the eggplants.
4. <u>Wash/Soak</u> the cauliflower.
5. <u>Wash</u> the asparagus.
6. <u>Trim off</u> the ends of the spring onions.
7. <u>Split</u> them down the middle.
8. <u>Scrub/Peel/Dice</u> the potatoes.
9. <u>Dice/Peel/Wash</u> the carrots.
10. <u>Make</u> a salad.
11. <u>Peel/Wash</u> the tomatoes.
12. <u>Chop</u> the onions fine.
13. <u>Boil</u> the corn.
14. <u>Prepare/Crush/Grind</u> the garlic.
15. <u>Cut</u> each head of cabbage in half.

Do Extension Activities
Activity 1
1. Carrot　　2. Celery　　3. Corn　　4. Cucumber
5. Eggplant　6. Lettuce　　7. Olive　　8. Pea
9. Potato　　10. Pumpkin　11. Tomato　12. Yam

Unit 5　Food Material II

Part A
Start you off
Activity 1

water melon

orange

strawberry

peach

lemon

apple

banana

lichee

pineapple

starfruit

coconut

honeydew melon

mango

pomegranate

papaya

cherry

Activity 2

FRUIT	VEGETABLE
cherry	cauliflower
pear	bean
plum	celery
grape	sweet pepper
apricot	turnip
tangerine	broccoli
pineapple	carrot
blueberry	

Activity 3

1. Put peaches into the fruit salad.
2. Wash the plums.
3. Put cream on the strawberry.
4. Peel the orange.
5. Boil the pears for five minutes.
6. Slice open the water melon.
7. Wash the grapes well.
8. Bring me some tangerines.
9. Mash up the bananas.
10. Serve the clean apricots.

Key to Exercises

Focus on language

Language Tips

Practice 1

14 fruits are mentioned.

apple, grapes, kiwi, berries, pineapple, orange, apricot, plum, banana, mangoes, papaya, avocado, purple plums, watermelon

Practice 2

VEGETABLES AND FRUITS	COLORS
Spinach	green
Sweet potatoes	red
Beans	green
Corn	yellow
Plums	red or purple
Watermelon	red
Onion	white or brown
Kiwi	yellowish green
Apricot	yellow
Manago	orange

Practice 3

1. Because they are nutritious.
2. Because fruits and vegetables are a natural source of energy and give the body many nutrients you need to keep going.
3. They contain great sources of many vitamins, minerals and other natural substances.
4. The best time to eat fruits is before dinner, because the sugars are burnt immediately, producing instant energy.
5. Open.

Give it a try

Do Extension Activities

Activity 1

1. Whatever you do, don't try to eat the <u>skin</u> of a banana!
2. Plums and peaches have large <u>pips</u>.
3. Grapes and bananas grow in <u>bunches</u>.
4. Grapes can be seeded or <u>seedless</u>.
5. Grapes have seeds, but lemons and limes have <u>stones</u>
6. Mangoes, lychees and starfruit are sometimes called tropical or <u>exotic</u> fruit.
7. Golden Delicious, Cox's, and Granny Smith are different <u>varieties</u> of apple.
8. A grapefruit is part of the same family as the orange, but much more <u>bitter</u>.

Activity 2

1. peaches	apples	plums	<u>pumpkin</u>	lychees
2. oranges	apricots	grapes	blackberries	<u>cabbage</u>
3. <u>pineapple</u>	peas	beans	aubergines	carrot
4. celery	eggplant	<u>tangerines</u>	cauliflower	asparagus
5. <u>potatoes</u>	coconut	watermelon	cherries	grapefruit
6. bananas	mangoes	green grapes	lemons	<u>onions</u>
7. melon	dates	strawberries	pears	<u>peppers</u>
8. papaya	peaches	starfruit	melon	<u>mushroom</u>

Part B
Start you off

Activity 1

Peel the banana.

Slice open the pineapple.

Peel/squeeze the orange.

Slice open the watermelon.

Peel the kiwi.

Squeeze the lemon.

Wash the grapes./Remove the seeds from the grapes.

Remove the seeds from the papaya.

Activity 2

1. Put the pineapple /apple / peach into the fruit salad.
2. Wash the pear / apple / grapes.
3. Soak the strawberries.
4. Put cream on the strawberries.
5. Peel the banana / orange / tangerine.
6. Boil the apricots.
7. Slice open the watermelon / pineapple.
8. Remove the seeds from the papaya.
9. Squeeze the orange / lemon / lime.
10. Mash up the banana.

Focus on Language

Handling Food

Language Tips

Practice 1

hands	Wash and dry thoroughly
raw food	Keep them away from cooked foods and ready-to-eat foods.
chopping boards	Wash and dry thoroughly and separate them for raw and cooked foods
knives	Wash and dry thoroughly
plates	Wash thoroughly
vegetables	Wash thoroughly
utensils	Wash and dry thoroughly

Practice 2

1. F 2. F 3. T 4. F 5. F 6. T

Practice 3

1. Use clean kitchen utensils not fingers for handling foods.
2. Keep raw and cooked foods apart at all times.
3. Wash hands, utensils — including chopping boards and knives — and surfaces thoroughly after preparing raw meat, fish, poultry and other raw foods.
4. Better use separate chopping boards for raw and cooked foods.
5. Root vegetables may contain harmful bacteria.
6. Avoid preparing food for yourself or others if you are ill, especially with vomiting and / or diarrhoea.

Key to Exercises

Give it a try
Do Extension Activities
Activity 1

1. Apple 2. Banana 3. Grapefruit 4. Grapes 5. Lemon
6. Lime 7. Melon 8. Peach, pear, plum 9. Raisin 10. Strawberry

Activity 2

1. A 2. B 3. C 4. C 5. B 6. A 7. C 8. B 9. C 10. A

Unit 6　Food Material III

Part A
Start You Off
Activity 2

1. slice a beef
2. season a lamb rack
3. wrap a beef
4. braise a beef
5. stew a veal
6. carve a lamb
7. sauté mutton
8. grill a steak

Focus on Language
Answers to the questions:

1. The tenderness of cooked steak is influenced by how much it is done.
2. Rare steaks still maintain their rawness and are very pink in color. Medium steaks are pink in the center, grayish brown at the surroundings. Well-done steaks are brown throughout and also tough to chew.
3. Omitted.

Language Tips

2. The ingredients needed to make beef or lamb dish

Practice 2

Name of the dish: sautéed mutton with scallion

200 grams of lamb slice　　1 tsp. ginger, minced
1 tbsp. sauce　　some salt and sugar
2 scallions　　1 tsp. vinegar
1 tsp. ground garlic

3. How to make a dish

Practice 1

1. No. He cooked the beef over medium heat.
2. He added water, salt and pepper.
3. Yes.

Practice 2

8 hours　　medium heat　　325-degree oven　　seasoning　　Serve over rice

Give It a Try
Task 1

Name of the dish: pepper steak
What are needed: beef sirloin, onion, soy sauce, vegetable oil, ground pepper
Work before cooking: slice the beef and onion
When to stop sautéing meat: until the pinkness is gone

How to treat pepper: add 1 teaspoon of freshly ground pepper

Time for simmering: 1—2 minutes

What to serve over: rice

Task 2

The correct order should be: 3, 2, 4, 1

Part B

Focus on Language

plastic bag   freezer   34° and 40°F   0°F or colder   −20°F

Language Tips

1. Tips on the preparation of materials

Practice 2

1. f   2. k   3. h   4. e   5. j   6. l   7. d   8. i   9. c   10. g   11. b   12. a

2. Tips on the process of making a dish

Practice 1

S: roast duck

C: salt and pepper

S: And what shall we do next

C: on all sides

S: Then shall we begin roasting

C: till the duck is pierced with a fork

S: What is the last step

C: remove meat from bones

Give It a Try

Task 1

Name of the dish: fried chicken

What are needed: flour, egg wash, vegetable oil and chicken

How to treat chicken: put it into the flour and lightly coat it

What should be cared about: The chicken will first sink to the bottom and then rise to the top.

How to see it is done: It should have a nice crunchy exterior.

Time for frying: 4—5 minutes

What to serve with: rice

Unit 7   Making a Meal

Part A

Activity 1

sweet pepper	fish	egg	olive oil
watermelon	lemon	mushroom	bacon
salmon	pineapple	peanut	sea cucumber
prawn	shellfish	butter	

Activity 2

chopping board	tea cup	fork	microwave
garlic squeezer	refrigerator	chopstick	cupboard
coffee pot	whisk	measuring cup	frying pan

Key to Exercises

tin opener　　　　　fish scaler　　　　　blender　　　　　oven

Focus on Language

1. Appetizer is any small, bite-size food served before a meal.

2. It's called hors d'oeuvre.

3. It can also apply to a first course served at the table.

Language Tips

1. Talking about the types of appetizers

Practice 3

1	土豆培根沙拉 Potato & Bacon Salad	黑椒牛柳 Sautéed Beef Fillet with Black Pepper	豆瓣鲈鱼 Sautéed Perch in Spicy Soybean Paste
2	咖喱鸡 Stewed Chicken with Curry	酸果/泡菜 relishes	香辣蟹 Sautéed Crab in Hot and Spicy Sauce
3	烧烤排骨 Barbecued Spare Rib	红烧海参 Braised Sea Cucumber in Soy Sauce	冷鸡肉卷 Chicken Galantine
4	清蒸闸蟹 Steamed River Crab	鹅肝酱 Pate de Foie Gras	煎比目鱼 Pan-fried Sole
5	兔肉批 Hare Pie	红酒烩鸡 Braised Chicken with Red Wine	海鲜意粉 Spaghetti with Seafood

土豆培根沙拉 Potato & Bacon Salad　　　酸果/泡菜 relishes　　　冷鸡肉卷 Chicken Galantine
鹅肝酱 Pate de Foie Gras　　　　　　兔肉批 Hare Pie

2. Discussing the ingredients

Practice 2

水果沙拉　　　strawberry 草莓　　　banana 香蕉　　　apple 苹果　　　salad dressing 沙拉酱
海鲜沙拉　　　prawn 对虾　　　　scallop 扇贝　　　lettuce 生菜/莴苣　salad dressing 沙拉汁
焗牡蛎　　　　oyster 牡蛎　　　　butter 黄油　　　white wine 白酒　　salt & pepper 盐、胡椒
鹅肝批　　　　goose liver 鹅肝　　red wine 红酒　　salt & pepper 盐、胡椒

Do Extension Activities

Activity 3

1. A canapé is a small, usually decorative food, held in the fingers and often eaten in one bite.

2. Because they are often served during cocktail hours.

3. It may also be referred to as finger food.

Activity 4

apple, pear, grape, sugar

butter, cream

onion

salt, pepper, soup

Part B

Start You Off

A: order　　　　　　　B: something, drink
A: soft, wine, beer, tea　　B: soup, tomato, egg

A: Certainly   B: jasmine
A: moment

Focus on Language

food   ingredients   meat   vegetables   boiling   flavor   broth

Language Tips

1. Discussing soup

   Practice 1

   胡萝卜茸汤 carrots puree soup (茸汤)
   奶油蘑菇汤 cream of mushroom soup (奶油汤)
   法式洋葱汤 French onion soup (蔬菜汤)
   鸡肉汤 chicken broth (浓肉汤)
   菜丝清汤 consommé julienne (清汤)
   龙虾汤 lobster bisque (海鲜汤)
   水果冷汤 cold fruit soup (冷汤)

   Practice 2

   1. Duck in Aweto Soup   虫草鸭块汤
   2. Tomato and Egg Soup   番茄蛋花汤
   3. Spare Rib and Turnip Soup   萝卜排骨汤
   4. Fish Fillet Soup   鱼片汤
   5. Fish Head and Fresh Mushroom Soup   鲜菌鱼头汤
   6. Sea Cucumber Soup, Shandong Style   山东海参汤
   7. Chinese Cabbage and Tofu Soup   白菜豆腐汤
   8. Borscht Soup   罗宋汤
   9. Shredded Pork and Preserved Vegetable Soup   榨菜肉丝汤
   10. Bamboo Fungus and White Fungus Soup   竹荪银耳汤

2. Preparing the ingredients

   Practice 2

Chilled Tomato and Red Sweet Pepper Soup	
Ingredients	**Steps of preparing the ingredients**
red sweet pepper	wash the red sweet pepper and remove the seeds
tomato	chop the tomato into slices
celery	peel the onion
onion	chop the celery and onion into dices
lemon	peel the lemon and blender it into juice

Oyster Soup	
Ingredients	**Steps of preparing the ingredients**
oyster	clean the oyster
butter	peel the tomato, onion and carrot
flour	chop tomato, onion carrot and celery into small dices
tomato	melt the butter in a pan
onion	mix the butter in flour, add oyster, white wine, salt and pepper

Key to Exercises

carrot	
celery	
white wine	
salt	
pepper	

3. Processing the preparation of the ingredients

Practice 1

apple	first step	rinse
	second step	peel
	third step	cut into slices/ dices
	fourth step	put into plate
mashed potato	first step	wash
	second step	boil
	third step	peel
	fourth step	smash
fish	first step	scale
	second step	open the stomach
	third step	take out the guts
	fourth step	rinse
minced garlic	first step	peel
	second step	crush
	third step	add salt
	fourth step	grind

Practice 2

A: 这些西红柿怎麼处理？   B: 先洗一下。
A: 然后呢？   B: 把根切掉。
A: 下一步呢？   B: 把西红柿放在开水里煮 15 秒。
A: 之后呢？   B: 马上放进凉水里。
A: 为什麼？   B: 这样容易剥皮。
A: 噢。我们用西红柿做什麼？   B: 西红柿汤。

Give It a Try

Task 1

A: times   wash   B: least
A: potatoes   B: have

Task 2

whisk—egg   peel—potato   scale—fish   crush—garlic

Do Extension Activities

Activity 1

1. There are mainly 7 kinds of soup in western cuisine.
2. The ingredients of western clear soups are different form one to another. So there are generally beef clear soup, chicken clear soup and fish clear soup.
3. According to the different ingredients and the ways of cooking, puree soup can be divided into two categories.

Activity 2

1. 师傅，怎麼处理莴苣呀？   把它们泡在盐水里。
2. 做汤需要放土豆吗？   不需要。
3. 我们今天是用冻豌豆还是用罐装的？   都不用。我们今天用新鲜的。

Activity 3

The first step:	wash the green pepper
The second step:	cut the green pepper open
The third step:	remove the seed
The fourth step:	stuff the peppers with meat
The last step:	cook the green pepper in tomato sauce.

Activity 4

Hot and Sour Soup 酸辣汤

Ingredients	Steps of Making Hot and Sour Soup
pork strips	1. put pork strips , mushrooms, bamboo shoots and ham into boiling water
dried mushrooms	2. heat for several minutes
bamboo shoots	3. add chicken broth, shrimp, soy sauce
ham	4. continue to simmer for another few more minutes
boiling water	5. add vinegar, salt and pepper, cornstarch
chicken broth	6. add the well-beaten egg into the soup
shrimp	7. stir well and serve
soy sauce	
vinegar	
salt	
black pepper	
cornstarch	
water	
egg	

Activity 5

I. tofu, gold carp, ham, mushroom, rape
   laver, dried shrimp, coriander, egg, cucumber

II.

A	B
tofu	豆腐
dried shrimp	虾米
ham	火腿
cucumber	黄瓜
gold carp	鲫鱼
mushroom	蘑菇
egg	鸡蛋
laver	紫菜
rape	油菜
coriander	香菜

Key to Exercises

Unit 8 Making a Dish

Part A
Focus on Language

French   Italian   eyes   same   appetite   dishes   ingredients   taste

Language Tips

1. Discussing the amount of ingredients needed

Practice 2

800g spinach	300g onion	56g bacon	40g flour
700ml fresh milk	0.12tsp salt	0.25tsp pepper	445g flour
30ml cream	20g minced garlic	5 pieces bay leave	

2. Ways of cooking

Practice 1

1. braise→e   2. poach→g   3. steam→c   4. barbecue→f
5. stew→a   6. sauté→d   7. bake→b

Practice 2

grill tuna fillet, **braise** sole fillet and scallop, **pan-fry** salmon fillet,
roast stuffed turkey, **barbecue** chicken feet, **deep-fry** bacon rolls,
stew beef, **bake** lobster with garlic, **steam** eel in black bean sauce
boil egg, **sauté** lettuce, **poach** king prawn

Practice 3

New Zealand Beef Tenderloin with King Prawn（新西兰牛排配明虾）

Ingredients

<u>beef</u> tenderloin, <u>king</u> prawn, rice, <u>potato</u> chips

asparagus, <u>lemon</u> juice, curry powder

carrot, <u>onion</u>, morel sauce（羊肚菌汁）

cream of white <u>wine</u> sauce

Proceed（制作）

Marinate(腌) beef tenderloin with <u>salt</u> and <u>pepper</u>.

Marinate king <u>prawn</u> with lemon juice.

<u>Fry</u> the rice with curry powder, <u>chop</u> onion and put it on plate.

<u>Pan-fry</u> the beef tenderloin to medium well, <u>put</u> it on
the rice and <u>pour</u> the morel sauce around it.

Pan-fry king prawn and put it <u>beside</u> the beef tenderloin,
<u>serve</u> with sauté vegetables, potato chips, etc.

<u>Pour</u> the cream of <u>white</u> wine sauce.

Give It a Try

Task 1

<u>700—800g</u> lobsters	<u>30ml</u> white wine	<u>0.5tsp</u> salt
<u>10</u> large shrimps	<u>1 litter</u> water	<u>2 pieces</u> bay leaves
<u>3 pounds</u> pork	<u>4 cups</u> water	

Do Extension Activities

Activity 1

lobster 700—800g   onion 150g   garlic 20g   mushroom 100g
butter 60g   flour 20g   white wine 30ml   fresh milk 80ml
cream 30ml   cheese 50g

Activity 2

braise	sea cucumber and mushroom
soft-fry	shrimp with egg
stir-fry	giant lobster in black bean sauce
deep-fry	shrimp meat balls
scramble	eggs with tomato
steam	fish
boil	seasonal vegetables
sauté	black fungus with red pepper
roast	turkey
barbecue	chicken wing
bake	beef

Activity 3

Marinate salmon with salt, pepper, white wine, sliced lemon and oregano.

Pan-fry salmon with olive oil to be medium and roast it to be done.

Put the salmon on plate, serve with the sliced vegetables, potatoes and asparagus.

Pour the saffron sauce.

Activity 4

　　For making Curry Paste, we need 80g shallots, 80g garlic slices, 40g ginger, 60g green chillies, 60g red chillies, 160g curry powder, 40g ginger powder, 20g chilli powder, 80g sugar, 2 bay leaves and 650g oil. Besides that, we still need 30g salt, 2 tsp chicken powder, 15g starch, 180g water, 30g oyster sauce, 30g sugar and 2tsp soy sauce.

Activity 5

法式蛙腿蜗牛

原料：蛙腿、蜗牛、球形茴香、面包、白葡萄酒、黄汁、混合香料、盐、胡椒

制作：(1)将球形茴香煮熟调味，切成扇形。

　　　(2)将蛙腿、蜗牛炒熟，加入白葡萄酒、黄汁、调味。

　　　(3)所有材料装盘，用烤面包、混合香料装饰即可。

Activity 6

1. French cuisine is very famous in the world.

2. French dinner usually starts with Appetizers.

3. It includes Appetizers, Soup, Seafood, Sorbet, Entrée, Barbeque, Salad, Dessert and Coffee.

Part B

Start You Off

Activity 1

1. Westerners have their own plate of food while in China the dishes are placed on the table and everybody shares.

2. Chinese hosts sometimes use their chopsticks to put food in your bowl or plate.

3. You can just say a polite "thank you" and leave the food there.

Activity 2

1. culture of cuisine	do their best	
2. Chinese host	chopsticks	sign of politeness
3. to do	to eat the food	

Key to Exercises

Focus on Language

1. rich flavor, delightful coloring
2. soy sauce, vinegar, wine, jams, spices
3. local dish, special cuisine, local snack

Language Tips

1. Discussing the time needed
   Practice 1
   1. an hour and a half
   2. five to six minutes
   3. 4 minutes and 30 seconds
   4. 2 or 3 minutes
   5. 50 minute to one hour

   Practice 2
   1. F   2. F   3. F   4. T

3. Discussing typical food
   Practice 1

Russian	Chicken Kiev
French	Goose Liver Pie
Italian	Caesar Salad
American	Hawaii Seafood Salad
English	London Broil
German	Boiled Pork with Sour Cabbage Berlin Style

   Practice 3
   1. Yes.
   2. They are Anhui, Cantonese, Fujian, Hunan, Jiangsu, Shandong, Sichuan, and Zhejiang cuisine.
   3. Roasted Suckling Pig is typical Cantonese cuisine; Hunan cuisine is well-known for its Peppery and Hot Chicken; Sichuan cuisine is famous for its Hot Pot.

Give It a Try

Task 2

originated, widespread, Asia, America, Europe, Africa, Beijing, Shanghai, Ten Great Traditions

Task 3

Today's Specialty:	Hawaii Crab
How to Prepare:	
first:	steam the crab,
next:	marinate the meat of the crab with mixed herbs, salt, pepper and white wine,
then:	mix the mashed potatoes and crab meat to make crab cake,
after that:	put the crab cake into the oven to be done,
at last:	sauté the chopped onion, add white wine, mint paste, cream and seasoning.

Do Extension Activities

Activity 1
1. 烤箱预热至200度，放入鸡烤10—15分钟，然后取出。
2. 烤羊肉时，你应该时不时地翻一翻。
3. 往锅里加两杯水，将鱼再蒸10分钟。

Activity 3

its wide selection of materials, cooking methods, seafood
domestic animals,   birds, seafood and vegetables

quick frying,   quick frying with corn flour,   stew braising,
roasting, boiling,   using sugar to make fruit,   honey
Braised Abalone with Shells,
Fried Sea Cucumber with Fistulous Onion,
Fragrant Calamus in Milk Soup
tasty, fresh

Activity 4

Yangzhou, Zhenjiang, Huaian
Yangtze River (Chang Jiang)
strictness, cleanliness, freshness, fine, cutting, cooking
lightness, freshness, sweetness, taste
Meat, Eel,

Activity 5

Dishes Mentioned
1. Bird' Nest Soup
2. Shark's Fin Soup
3. Beijing Roast Duck
4. Sea Cucumber
5. Hot Pot
Steps of Preparing and Serving Beijing Roast Duck
1. clean the duck,
2. plug and fill it with water,
3. hook the duck on a spit in a huge, round doorless oven,
4. bring it to the table and cut it into thin slices,
5. dip the chopped cucumber and scallion into sweet soybean paste,
6. put them on a small, thin pancake with duck slices,
7. wrap the pancake into a roll and then serve.

Unit 9 Dessert

Part A
Start You Off

Activity 1

1. cake   2. muffin   3. apple pie   4. donut
5. croissant   6. bun   7. tiramisu   8. plait bread
9. toast   10. pudding   11. egg tart   12. ice cream

Activity 2

1. glass mixing bowls   2. balloon whisk   3. large round cake tin
4. electric hand mixer   5. scales   6. large square cake tin
7. measuring jug   8. measuring spoons   9. cake boards
10. pastry brush   11. pre-cut greaseproof paper tin liners 12. scissors
13. wooden mixing spoons   14. wire rack   15. sieve
16. oven gloves   17. plastic spatula   18. metal spoon

Focus on Language

Listening

CAKES

1. cakes 2. birthday. recipes 3. wedding 4. cake
5. Fruit cake 6. decorated 7. sponge

2. **Lining cake tins**

   Practice 1

   Lining Cake Tins

   Fill in the blanks with the word that you will hear on the tape.

   (1) lining cake tins (2) sticking (3) turn out (4) shape
   (5) Quick-mix (6) layer (7) rich (8) base

   Practice 3

   2—4—1—3—5

Part B

Start You Off

Activity 1

1. sponge cake 2. Swiss roll 3. Madeira cake
4. black forest gateau 5. mocha-hazelnut battenberg 6. angel food cake
7. panforte 8. sachertorte 9. cheesecake with fresh fruits

Activity 2

1. food colourings 2. piping nozzles 3. piping bag 4. icing turntable
5. cake pillars 6. frill cutter 7. textured rolling pin

Focus on Language

Listening

1. dark chocolate tiny slices 2. saturated fat rich flavour
3. creamy fresh fruit decoration 4. chopped nuts syrup
5. classic egg yolks snowy white

Language Tips

2. **Decorating with chocolate**

   Practice 2

   1. Chocolate 2. powdered 3. liquid 4. plastic container 5. ready to use

Give It a Try

Task 1

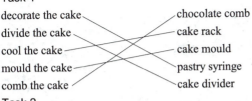

Task 2

1. Mix 2. Brush 3. Put on 4. Decorate/Garnish 5. Cut into

Unit 10 Food Safety

Part A

Start You Off

Activity 1

1. fly 2. cockroach 3. mouse 4. rat

Activity 2

Preparing — is the series of activities performed on food products before cooking.

Cooking — is the point at which heat is applied to food, to change its color, odor, etc.

Holding — is a critical control point particularly in food service operations that prepare products well in advance of service.

Focus on Language
Listening
(1) uniforms (2) caps (3) chef's hats
(4) hair nets (5) tasting of food (6) Hand-washing
(7) Single-use gloves (8) unauthorized person

Language Tips

2. Factors affecting bacterial reproduction
Practice
1. Moisture, oxygen level, PH level, time, and temperature factors.
2. Adding sugar or salt, drying, or freezing.
3. A PH between 6.6 and 7.5.

3. Foodborne infections and intoxications
Practice 2

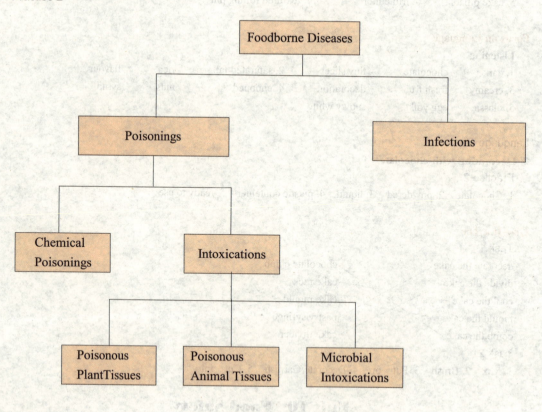

Give It a Try
Task 2
1. Cleaning(washing) and peeling vegetables, trimming meat, dicing, chopping, cutting and assembling raw ingredients.

2. Soil-grown vegetables and fresh fish.
3. Cooking is the point at which heat is applied to food to change its color, odor, texture, taste, appearance, and nutritional value.
   Holding is a critical control point panticularly in food service operation that prepare products well in advance of service. Menu items may be held hot or cold. Holding times should be as short as possible to maintain product quality and reduce food safety hazards. Holding temperatures must also be monitored carefully.

Do Extension Activities
Activity 1
(1) insects　　(2) rodents　　(3) food　　(4) preventive　　(5) pesticides
(6) food supply　　(7) breeding sites　　(8) garbage　　(9) cleaning up　　(10) damp

Part B
Start You Off
Activity 1
(1) break down　　(2) odor　　(3) color
(4) texture　　(5) appearance　　(6) taste
(7) temperatures　　(8) times　　(9) Excessive delays
(10) sanitation standards

Language Tips
1. Food poisoning
   Practice 3
   1. in　　2. from　　3. in　　4. out

Unit One   Kitchen Introduction

Part A
Focus on Language

Conversation

Listen to the conversation and read after it. Then try to find the answers to the questions.

Tapescript

A = Aribella   B = Bristol

B: So, Aribella, tell me about your family. Have you got any brothers or sisters?

A: Yeah. I've got three sisters but no brothers.

B: Three sisters. What are their names?

A: Well, Ann is the eldest; Cindy is the second eldest one; and Ellen is the youngest.

B: And what do they do?

A: Ann is twenty-three, she is married and has two children, and they keep her pretty busy. Cindy, the second oldest, is in college like me. She's studying computer science. And the other one, Ellen, is still in high school.

B: And what about your dad? What does he do for living?

A: Oh, he's a doctor, he loves his work and thinks it is very rewarding.

B: Oh, really? And your mom? Does she work, too?

A: Yeah, she's a journalist. She works for BEIJING YOUTH DAILY.

Part B
Focus on Language

Listening

Listen to the recording and fill in the blanks with the missing words you will hear.

Tapescript

Personal Health Cleanliness and Safety in the Kitchen

1. Hands must be thoroughly washed before starting work, after handling food, after smoking, after using the toilet and after using a handkerchief or tissue. The hand sink in the production area must be used for hand washing. The sink in the restroom must be used after using the restroom facilities. Hands must be washed with hot soapy water for a minimum of 20 seconds and dried with a paper towel.

2. All cuts must be bandaged with waterproof protectors, and watertight disposable gloves should be worn.

3. Kitchen staff with open lesions, infected wounds, sore throats or any communicable diseases shall not be permitted to work in the kitchen.

4. No eating or drinking permitted in the kitchen area. No use of tobacco products allowed in the kitchen.

5. Kitchen staff shall be clean and well groomed. Clothing should be made of a washable fabric. No open-toed shoes are to be worn in the kitchen.
6. All the kitchen staff is to wear hair restraints provided by the kitchen. This includes the use of both hair and beard nets as necessary.
7. Personal belongings must be kept out of food preparation and storage areas. All personal belongings are to be stored in the designated area or off premises.
8. Remove all insecure jewelry that might fall into food or equipment. Remove hand jewelry when manipulating food by hand.

Unit 2 Kitchen Facilities

Part A
Focus on Language

Listening

Listen to the passage and try to find the answers to the questions. Then put them in the table below.

Tapescript

Kitchen is a relatively independent place, known as what we call the heart of the entire operation. The real production takes place in this space. Known as a part of the back of the house, kitchen spreads over several rooms or areas. The function spaces in the kitchen can be categorized into three areas: cooking area where the final products come out; preparing and cutting space where the initial processing, including cutting, dish arranging, etc., is done; auxiliary area which includes storage space such as pantry, refrigerator, etc., dish washing area, and changing closet, which serves as transition area.

As a matter of fact, the area of a kitchen is crucial for a restaurant operation because it influences work efficiency and product quality

Give It a Try
Task 2

Listen to the recording and complete the following passage with the missing words.

Tapescript

Where should we put the refrigerators in the kitchen? Refrigerators should not be placed either close to cooking area, or washing area to prevent power failure due to heat and water. The materials used for the equipment in the kitchen should be of water proof because kitchen is a wet and humid place. Also materials should not be flammable(易燃的) for fire is indispensable(不可缺少的) in the kitchen.

Do Extension Activities
Activity 3

Listen to the following passage and write down the points according to the requirements.

Tapescript

Storage areas will vary according to the types of foods and beverages being stored and the temperatures required for their storage. Storage will be needed for dry, refrigerated, and frozen goods in addition to beverages and nonfood supplies. Most restaurants have two kinds of storage areas for food: dry storage and refrigerator-

freezer.

Dry storage areas are used for foods and various supplies to be kept at a temperature range of 50° F to 70°F (10°C to 21°C). The dry storeroom usually contains shelves on which items are arranged so that the foods most often used are the easiest to reach. Adequate ventilation (n. 通风) is needed for such foods as root vegetables or unripe (a. 未熟的) fruits. Certain supplies, such as linens, towels, paper goods, glassware, silverware and furniture may also be placed in dry storage areas.

Refrigerator-freezer areas are needed for products that have to be stored at the temperatures of 35°F to 40°F (1.7°C to 4.4°C) and -10°F to -20°F (-23°C to -28.9°C) respectively.

Part B
Give It a Try
Task 1

Listen to the following short conversations and write down the answers to what the Vegetable Chef is asking the Commis Cook to do.

Tapescript

Conversation 1

Commis Cook:	What are we going to do?
Vegetable Chef:	We are going to make a salad.
Commis Cook:	What shall we start with?
Vegetable Chef:	The spring onions.
Commis Cook:	What shall I do first?
Vegetable Chef:	Wash the spring onions.
Commis Cook:	And then?
Vegetable Chef:	Trim off both ends.
Commis Cook:	Anything else?
Vegetable Chef:	Yes. Split the spring onions down the middle.
Commis Cook:	With my cook's knife?
Vegetable Chef:	Of course.

Conversation 2

Commis Cook:	Shall I peel the garlic now?
Vegetable Chef:	Yes, please.
Commis Cook:	How shall I prepare the garlic?
Vegetable Chef:	Crush the garlic and then grind it.
Commis Cook:	And add the salt to the garlic?
Vegetable Chef:	That's right. We will mix the garlic with butter.
Commis Cook:	So we are making garlic butter today.
Vegetable Chef:	That's correct.

Conversation 3

Commis Cook:	What shall I do?
Vegetable Chef:	Wash these cucumbers.
Commis Cook:	And peel them?
Vegetable Chef:	Yes, please.
Commis Cook:	And then what?

Vegetable Chef:	Slice the cucumbers up.
Commis Cook:	For salad?
Vegetable Chef:	That's right. For cucumber salad.

Conversation 4

Commis Cook:	Shall I wash the cauliflower?
Vegetable Chef:	Yes, please. Wash it well.
Commis Cook:	All right. Cauliflower is always dirty.
Vegetable Chef:	Soak the cauliflower in salt water.
Commis Cook:	For how many minutes?
Vegetable Chef:	Thirty minutes will be enough.
Commis Cook:	How shall I cook the cauliflower?
Vegetable Chef:	Boil it in water with lemon juice.
Commis Cook:	Why?
Vegetable Chef:	The lemon juice will keep it white.

Task 3

Listen to the following conversation and complete the chart below with the proper names of different knives for preparing food and their functions according to the recording.

Tapescript

Commis:	What are these knives for?
Chef:	Well, this is a boning knife. The boning knife is used to remove bones from meat.
Commis:	What is this funny little knife for?
Chef:	It's an oyster knife. It's for opening oyster shells.
Commis:	What do you want me to do now?
Chef:	Carve the roast.
Commis:	What kind of knife shall I use?
Chef:	Use a carving knife.
Commis:	What shall I do now?
Chef:	Prepare some cheese for the cheese board.
Commis:	How shall I cut it?
Chef:	Use this big cheese knife with a double handle.

Unit 3   Condiments

Part A
Focus on Language

Listen to the tape and decide whether the following statements are true

Tapescript

  Condiment is a prepared edible substance or mixture, often preserved or fermented, usually used in relatively small quantities. Condiments are most often placed at the table to make food more suitable to the diner's taste. There are many kinds of condiments, for instance, salty, sweet, spicy, pickled condiments, compound sauces and so on.

Language Tips

1. Classifying condiments

Practice 1

Listen to the tape and answer the following questions.

Tapescript

Salty Condiment

Condiments fall into five nonexclusive categories. The first is salt, the earliest and most important condiment employed by humans. In addition to its presence on tables around the world, salt is often a constituent ingredient in many other condiments. It is employed on a wide range of foods, including vegetables, meats, fish, and poultry. Salt is a major preservative and today is commonly found in most processed foods.

Practice 2

Listen to the tape and complete the following statements.

Tapescript

Sweet Condiments

The second most common condiment is sugar or other sweeteners, such as honey or maple syrup. Sugar and honey are used directly in everything from bitter beverages such as tea, to a topping for breakfast cereals. Sugar and honey are also employed in making other condiments such as jams, jellies, marmalades and are used on bread, rolls and in pastries. Maple syrup is commonly used on pancakes.

Give It a Try

Task 1

Listen to the tape and answer the following questions.

Tapescript

Pickled Condiments

A third category of condiments is pickled foods, which date back to the ancient world in Europe as well as Asia. Common pickled foods used as condiments today include ginger, chutney and cucumbers. Almost all vegetables have been pickled and used as condiments in some form. They are served whole, in slices, or diced. Sliced and diced pickles are frequently used on sandwiches.

Task 2

Listen to the tape and fill in the blanks.

Tapescript

Spicy or Hot Condiments

A fourth condiment category are those spicy or hot foods, such as black pepper, chili pepper, mustard, garlic, horse-radish and onions. A product of Asia, black pepper is commonly served from shakers throughout the western world in a dried state and is usually ground into coarse or fine state before consumption.

Do Extension Activities

Activity 1

Listen to the tape and write out the missing information.

Tapescript

Compound sauces are also regarded as condiments. This kind of condiments include ketchup, Worcestershire sauce, fish sauces, soy sauce, salad dressings, curries, and barbecue sauces. The earliest known compound sauces which were made of fish were well accepted in widely separated regions, such as in the ancient Mediterranean and Southeast Asia.

Activity 2

Listen to the information of Russian Mustard and write it down.

Tapescript

Russian Mustard
- Smooth and Lasting
- Served as spread or dressing
- Hot but sweet
- No preservatives

Activity 4

Listen to the conversation and write out the missing information.

Tapescript

A: There are many condiments used in the western cuisine, you know.

B: Of course I know. But can you give me an example?

A: Sure. For instance Worcestershire sauce, vinegar, tomato paste, curry, mustard and so on.

B: I was told that vinegar has a big variety. Is that true?

A: Yes, it's true.

B: So, what are the different vinegars?

A: They are balsamic vinegar, champagne vinegar, herb vinegar, tarragon vinegar, wine vinegar, sherry vinegar, apple vinegar, aromatic vinegar and white vinegar.

Part B

Focus on Language

Listen to the tape and fill in the blanks.

Tapescript

Spices

There are about 35 spices which can be broadly classified into 6 groups, based upon the parts of the plants which they are obtained, namely (i) rhizomes and root spices, (ii) bark spices, (iii) leaf spices, (iv) flower spices, (v) fruit spices, and (vi) seed spices.

Language Tips

1. Discussing the culinary uses of spices

Practice 1

Listen to the tape and answer the following questions.

Tapescript

Bay Leaf

Bay leaves are spices and widely used throughout the world. It may be best used in soups, sauces, stews. It is an appropriate seasoning for fish, meat and poultry. Bay leaf is often included as a pickling spice.

Practice 2

Listen to the tape and answer the following questions.

Tapescript

Pepper

Pepper is best ground directly onto food. With hot food it is best to add pepper well towards the end of the cooking process, to preserve its aroma. White pepper is used in white sauces rather than black pepper, which would give the sauce a speckled appearance. Green peppercorns can be mashed with garlic, cinnamon or to make a spiced butter or with cream to make a fresh and attractive sauce for fish.

2. Talking about the flavor of spices

Practice 1

Listen to the tape, write out the flavor of the following spices and make similar conversations as the example given above.

Tapescript

Nutmeg is nutty, warm and slightly sweet.
Cloves are sweetly pungent and strongly aromatic.
Cinnamon is warm and aromatic.

Practice 2

Listen to the tape and decide whether the following statements are true or false.

Tapescript

Black pepper is very pungent and fiery.
White pepper is less pungent.
Green pepper is milder with a cleaner, fresher flavor.

Give It a Try

Task 1

Listen to the tape and fill in the blanks.

Tapescript

Cinnamon

Cinnamon is used more in dessert dishes. It is commonly used in cakes and other baked goods, milk and rice puddings, chocolate dishes and fruit desserts, particularly apples and pears. It is common in many Middle Eastern and North African dishes. Cinnamon is used in flavoring lamb.

Do Extension Activities
Activity 1
Listen to the tape and write out the kind of meat and vegetables working well with thyme.

Tapescript

Thyme

Thyme works well with veal, lamb, beef, poultry, fish, sausages, soups, bread, herbed butters, herbed mayonnaise, and mustard. Use it with tomatoes, onions, cucumbers, carrots, eggplant, leeks, mushrooms, asparagus, green beans, broccoli, sweet peppers, potatoes, spinach, corn, peas, cheese, eggs, and rice.

Activity 2
Listen to the tape and match the words in column A with those in column B and in column C.

Tapescript

Aprika, which mainly produces in Hungary, is slightly sweet, while oregano originating in Europe, west and south Asia, is bitter and strongly aromatic. With Indonesia, the Philippines, India as its chief places of production, betelnut is very aromatic and slightly bitter.

Activity 3
Listen to the tape and write out the missing information.

Tapescript

The basic classification of spices is as follows: First, leaves or branches of aromatic plants, for example, bay leaf, tarragon, thyme, oregano, chervil. Second, ripened fruits or seeds of plants. Examples include dill, fennel, coriander, mustard, black pepper etc. Third, roots or bulbs of certain plants. Examples include garlic, onion, celery and ginger.

Unit 6 Food Material III

Part A
Focus on Language

Tapescript

The tenderness of cooked steak is influenced by how much it is done. Depending on the time for which the steak is cooked, it may be raw, very rare, rare, medium rare, medium, medium well-done and well-done. Rare steaks are exposed to the flame for a very short time. They still maintain their rawness and are very pink in color. Rarely done steaks maintain their original beefy flavors, but they are not very healthy as they still contain microorganisms. As the cooking time increases, the pinkness of steak gets converted to brownness and its juiciness also reduces. Medium steaks are pink in the center, grayish brown at the surroundings. Well-done steaks are brown throughout and also tough to chew.

Language Tips

2. The ingredients needed to make beef or lamb dish

Practice 2

Tapescript

A. What do you use to make sautéed mutton with scallion?

B. We need 200 grams of lamb slice, 2 scallions, 1 teaspoon of ground garlic, 1 teaspoon of minced ginger, 1 tablespoon of sauce, 1 teaspoon of vinegar and some salt and sugar.

3. How to make a dish

Practice 1

Tapescript

C=Chef   S=Student

C: Cook the beef over medium heat.

S: For how long?

C: Ten minutes.

　(After ten minutes)

S: Ten minutes are up.

C: Add water, salt and pepper.

S: I will heat it to boiling.

C: Then reduce the heat. Cover and simmer the beef.

S: For how long?

C. Five to ten minutes.

Practice 2

Tapescript

　　For preparation, you need to cut the lamb into cubes and marinate it in wine for 8 hours. To start, you need to cook onion and garlic in butter. Stir in curry powder. Then drain lamb from wine and add it to onion mixture, cook covered over medium heat for 10 minutes, stirring frequently. Add salt, soup, milk and wine. Then cook in 325-degree oven for 2 hours. Stir in sour cream and heat. Choose the seasoning per your taste. Serve over rice.

Give It a Try

Task 1

Tapescript

　　Today we are going to make an easy pepper steak. These are the ingredients: 1 pound of beef sirloin, 1 onion, 2 tablespoons of soy sauce and vegetable oil, 1 teaspoon of ground pepper. Slice meat into thin strips. Slice onion. Heat 2 tablespoons vegetable oil in frying pan. Sauté onions for 1 minute and add meat. Sauté until pinkness is gone. Add soy sauce. Add 1 teaspoon of freshly ground pepper. Stir and cover. Simmer 1 to 2 minutes on low heat. Serve over rice.

Part B
Focus on Language

Tapescript

Store your seafood in the refrigerator if you intend to use it within two days after purchase. In case you will not use your seafood within two days after purchase, wrap it in moisture-proof paper or plastic wrap, place it in a heavy plastic bag, or put it in an airtight, rigid container, and store it in the freezer. Keep the temperature of the refrigerator between 34° and 40°F, and of your freezer at 0°F or colder, as close to -20°F as possible.

Language Tips
2. Tips on the process of making a dish
Practice 1

Tapescript
S=Student   C=Chef
S: We are going to make a roast duck. Where shall we start with?
C: Wash and dry the bird. Rub with flour and sprinkle all over with salt and pepper.
S: And what shall we do next?
C: Melt the butter in a pan and brown the duck on all sides.
S: Then shall we begin roasting?
C: Yes, roast the duck in an oven at 350 degrees for 45 minutes to 1 hour, uncovered, till the duck is pierced with a fork.
S: Which side should be up during the roasting?
C: The breast side of the duck.
S: What is the last step?
C: Finally, remove meat from bones and pour gravy in pan over meat.

Give It a Try
Task 1

Tapescript

I'm going to show you the procedure for fried chicken. We have seasoned flour, seasoned egg wash, and heated vegetable oil which must be heated to at least 350 degrees but no more then 400 degrees. We are going to take our piece of chicken. We are going to put it into the flour and lightly coat it. We are going to throw it into the egg wash. Move it around to get it nice and saturated. Then we are going to throw that directly into our fryer. Be careful because as you could see it has sunk to the bottom and as it loses moisture through the cooking process it would rise to the top. It would take 4-5 minutes to cook in the deep fryer and when it is done it has a nice crunchy exterior. And that is our fried chicken which has a wonderful golden texture. It is served with rice.

Unit 7　Making a Meal

Part A
Focus on Language
Listen to the tape and answer the following questions.

Tapescript
Appetizer, which is also called hors d'oeuvre in French, is any small, bite-size food served before a meal. It can also apply to a first course served at the table.

Do Extension Activities
Activity 3
Listen to the tape and answer the following questions.

Tapescript
A canapé is a small, usually decorative food, held in the fingers and often eaten in one bite. Because canapés are often served during cocktail hours, they are often either salty or spicy in order to encourage guests to drink more. A canapé may also be referred to as finger food although not all finger foods are canapés.

Activity 4
Listen to the tape and put the following ingredients of different appetizers into the right place.

Tapescript

Fruit Cocktail
apple, pear, grape, sugar, strawberry, lemon juice

Smoked Salmon Canapés
toast, smoked salmon, butter, cream, cheese powder, lemon juice, salt

Pate de Foie Gras
foie gras, goose oil, fresh cream, sherry, onion, bay leaf,
thyme, nutmeg, salt, pepper, soup

Part B
Start You Off
Listen to the tape and complete the following conversation.

Tapescript
A: Are you ready to order now?
B: I want to have something to drink first.
A: Do you want soft drink, wine, beer or tea?
B: I want to have soup. Do you have tomato and egg soup?
A: Certainly.
B: Ok. I'll have the soup and some tea, jasmine tea, please.
A: One moment, sir.

Tapescript

Focus on Language
Listen to the tape and fill in the blanks.

Tapescript

Soup

Soup is a food that is made by combining ingredients such as meat or vegetables in stock or hot/boiling water, until the flavor is extracted, forming a broth.

Language Tips

2. Preparing the ingredients

Practice 2

Listen to the tape about "Chilled Tomato and Red Sweet Pepper Soup", "Oyster Soup" and put all the Ingredients and the Steps of preparing the ingredients given below into the right place in the chart.

Tapescript

Chilled Tomato and Red Sweet Pepper Soup

You have to make a lot of preparations for *Chilled Tomato and Red Sweet Pepper Soup*. You have to wash the red sweet pepper and remove the seeds; chop the tomato into slices; peel the onion; chop the celery and onion into dices; peel the lemon and blender it into juice.

Oyster Soup

There are lots of things to do. For instance, clean the oyster and peel the tomato, onion and carrot; chop them and celery into small dices; melt the butter in a pan; mix the butter in flour; add oyster, white wine, salt and pepper.

Give It a Try

Task 1

Listen to the conversation and write out the missing words.

Tapescript

A: For how many times do I have to wash the cauliflower?

B: At least three times.

A: How about potatoes?

B: You don't have to.

Do Extension Activities

Activity 3

There are several steps in preparing the green pepper for a dish. Listen to the tape and write out the steps.

Tapescript

The first step: wash the green pepper
The second step: cut the green pepper open
The third step: remove the seed
The fourth step: stuff the peppers with meat

The last step: cook the green pepper in tomato sauce.

Activity 4

Listen to the tape, write out the missing information and then make a conversation talking about it.

Tapescript

Hot and Sour Soup 酸辣汤

First of all, put pork strips, mushrooms, bamboo shoots and ham into boiling water. Heat for several minutes. Add chicken broth, shrimp, soy sauce and continue to simmer for another few more minutes. Then add vinegar, salt and pepper, cornstarch. And at last add the well-beaten egg into the soup. Stir well and serve.

Activity 5

The following are two kinds of soups. Listen to the tape and write out the ingredients for each of them.

Tapescript

Today we are going to make two soups. The ingredients for *Gold Carp and Tofu Soup* are tofu, gold carp, ham, mushroom and rape. The ingredients for *Egg Drop Soup* are laver, dried shrimp, coriander, egg and cucumber.

Unit 8   Making a Dish

Part A   Making Western Food

Focus on Language

Listen and write out the missing words.

Tapescript

French and Italian cuisines are very appealing to the eyes; at the same time, they are very stimulating to the appetite. The colorful dishes are full of natural ingredients and in good taste.

Language Tips

1. Discussing the amount of ingredients needed

Practice 2

Listen and write out the amount of ingredients.

Tapescript

800g	spinach
300g	onion
56g	bacon
40g	flour
700ml	fresh milk
0.12tsp	salt
0.25tsp	pepper
445g	flour
30ml	cream
20g	minced garlic

5 pieces   bay leave

2. Ways of cooking

Practice 2

Listen and write out the different ways of cooking in the proper place according to what you hear from the tape.

Tapescript

grill	tuna fillet
braise	sole fillet and scallop
pan-fry	salmon fillet
roast	stuffed turkey
barbecue	chicken feet
deep-fry	bacon rolls
stew	beef
bake	lobster with garlic
steam	eel in black bean sauce
boil	egg
sauté	lettuce
poach	king prawn

Practice 3

Listen to the tape and write out the missing information

Tapescript

Today we are going to make a New Zealand dish. The ingredients we need are: beef tenderloin, king prawn, rice, potato chips, asparagus, lemon juice, curry powder, carrot, onion, morel sauce, cream of white wine sauce. The way we cook it is like this: Marinate beef tenderloin with salt and pepper. Marinate king prawn with lemon juice. Fry the rice with curry powder, chop onion and put it on plate. Pan-fry the beef tenderloin to medium well, put it on the rice and pour the morel sauce around it. Pan-fry king prawn and put it beside the beef tenderloin, serve with sautéd vegetables, potato chips, etc. At last, pour the cream of white wine sauce.

Give It a Try

Task 1

Listen and write out the amount of ingredients needed.

Tapescript

700-800g lobsters
30ml white wine
0.5tsp salt
10 large shrimps
1 litter water
2 pieces bay leaves
3 pounds pork
4 cups water

Do Extension Activities

Activity 1

Listen to the tape, write out the ingredients and the amount of ingredients needed for Baked Lobster with Cheese and White Wine Sauce.

Tapescript

We are going to make Baked Lobster with Cheese and White Wine Sauce today. The ingredients we have to prepare are: 700-800g lobster, 150g onion, 20g garlic, 100g mushroom, 60g butter, 20g flour, 30ml white wine, 80ml fresh milk, 30ml cream and 50g cheese.

Activity 2

Listen and match the words in column A with that in column B.

Tapescript

braise sea cucumber and mushroom
soft-fry shrimp with egg
stir-fry giant lobster in black bean sauce
deep-fry shrimp meat balls
scramble eggs with tomato
steam fish
boil seasonal vegetables
sauté black fungus with red pepper
roast turkey
barbecue chicken wing
bake beef

Activity 3

Listen to the tape, write out the missing words and then rearrange the statements into the right order.

Tapescript

Now I'm going to tell you how to make Grilled Salmon in Norwegian Style. **Marinate** salmon with salt, pepper, white wine, sliced lemon and oregano. **Pan-fry** salmon with olive oil to be medium and roast it to be done. **Put** the salmon on plate, serve with the sliced vegetables, potatoes and asparagus. **Pour** the saffron sauce.

Activity 6

Listen and answer the following questions.

Tapescript

French cuisine is one of the most famous cuisines in the world. Very formal French dinner begins with Appetizers, and then Soup, Seafood, Sorbet, Entrée, Barbeque, Salad, Dessert and Coffee.

Part B
Start You Off

Activity 1

Listen to the Table Manners and answer the following questions.

Tapescript

The main difference between Chinese and western eating habits is that unlike the West, where everyone has their own plate of food, in China the dishes are placed on the table and everybody shares. Chinese are very proud of their culture of cuisine and will do their best to show their hospitality. Sometimes the Chinese host uses his chopsticks to put food in your bowl or plate. This is a sign of politeness. The appropriate thing to do would be to eat the food. If you feel uncomfortable with this, you can just say a polite "thank you" and leave the food there.

Activity 2

Listen to the Table Manners again and complete the statements.

Tapescript

The main difference between Chinese and western eating habits is that unlike the west, where everyone has their own plate of food, in China the dishes are placed on the table and everybody shares. Chinese are very proud of their culture of cuisine and will do their best to show their hospitality. Sometimes the Chinese host uses his chopsticks to put food in your bowl or plate. This is a sign of politeness. The appropriate thing to do would be to eat the food. If you feel uncomfortable with this, you can just say a polite "thank you" and leave the food there.

Focus on Language

Listen to the tape and complete the following statements.

Tapescript

Chinese cooking has a long history and is famous all over the world for its rich flavor and delightful coloring. It was the Chinese who invented the technique of making and using soy sauce, vinegar, wine, jams and spices during the Yin-Zhou period, some 3000 years ago and very Chinese local dish, special cuisine and local snack has its own characteristics.

Language Tips

1. Discussing the time needed

Practice 1

Listen and complete the following statements.

Tapescript

1. Roast the chicken for an hour and a half.
2. Sauté the mushroom for five to six minutes.
3. Grill the mutton for 4 minutes and 30 seconds.
4. Deep-fry the fish in the hot oil for 2 or 3 minutes.
5. Braise the beef for 50 minute to one hour.

Practice 2

Listen and decide whether the following statements are true or false.

Tapescript

1. Bake the bread for about 13 minutes until it turns golden brown.
2. Preheat the oven to 190°C. Bake the skewers for 14 minutes and then serve.
3. Stew the beef for about 40 minutes, then add some water and stew it for another 14 minutes.
4. Boil the egg for 8 minutes and 30 seconds.

3. Discussing typical food

Practice 1

Listen to the tape and match the information.

Tapescript

A: What is typical Russian food, chef?
B: Borscht Moscow style, Chicken Kiev and so on.
A: How about French, Italian and American food?
B: Goose Liver Pie, Snails in Shell Herb Butter are world famous French food. Caesar Salad, Fried Pork Chop Milanese, Spaghetti are well-known Italian food and Hawaii Seafood Salad, Waldorf Salad are typical American food.
A: And what are the specialties of English and German Food?
B: London Broil and Boiled Pork with Sour Cabbage Berlin Style.
A: I see.

Practice 3

Listen to the tape and answer the following questions.

Tapescript

Chinese cuisine has a long history and it has become world-famous. There are eight main regional cuisines. Bird's Nest Soup is typical Shandong Cuisine. Sichuan Cuisine is famous for its Hot Pot. Roasted Suckling Pig is typical Cantonese cuisine item. Fuotiaoqiang is Fujian local specialty. Mandarin Fish is something typical of Huaiyang cuisine. Zhejiang cuisine is famous for Sour West Lake Fish. Hunan cuisine is well-known for its Peppery and Hot Chicken and Anhui cuisine is famous for Huangshan Braised Pigeon.

Give It a Try

Task 2

Listen to the tape and write out the missing words.

Tapescript

Chinese cuisine originated from the various regions of China and has become widespread in many other parts of the world—from East Asia to North America, Australia, Western Europe and Southern Africa. There are eight main regional cuisines, Anhui, Cantonese, Fujian, Hunan, Jiangsu, Shandong, Sichuan and Zhejiang. Occasionally Beijing cuisine and Shanghai cuisine are also cited along with the eight regional styles as the Ten Great Traditions.

Tapescript

Task 3
Listen to the conversation, fill in the chart and make a conversation talking about today's special dish.

Tapescript

A: What is our specialty today, chef?

B: Our specialty today is Hawaii Crab.

A: Can you tell me how to make it?

B: Sure. Steam crab first. Marinate the meat of the crab with mixed herbs, salt, pepper and white wine. Then mix the mashed potatoes and crab meat to make crab cake. After that put it into the oven to be done. Sauté the chopped onion, add white wine, mint paste, cream and seasoning.

Do Extension Activities

Activity 3
Listen to the tape about typical food, complete the following statements and make a conversation talking about Shandong Dishes.

Tapescript

Shandong Dishes

Shandong cuisine is famous for its wide selection of materials, cooking methods and seafood. The raw material used are mainly domestic animals and birds, seafood and vegetables. The masterful cooking techniques include quick frying, quick frying with corn flour, stew braising, roasting and boiling, using sugar to make fruit, and crystallizing with honey. Famous Shandong dishes are Braised Abalone with Shells, Fried Sea Cucumber with Fistulous Onion, and Fragrant Calamus in Milk Soup. The dishes are tasty and fresh.

Activity 4
Listen to the tape, complete the following statements and use the information given to make a conversation.

Tapescript

Huaiyang Dishes

Huaiyang dishes mainly consist of Yangzhou, Zhenjiang and Huaian cuisine originated in water villages south of the Yangtze River, and are characterized by the strictness in material selection, the cleanliness and freshness of its ingredients as well as the fine workmanship in cutting, matching, cooking, and arranging. Lightness, freshness, sweetness and mildness of taste are the features of these dishes. Special attention is paid to retaining the ingredient of natural juices and flavors. Famous dishes are Crystal Meat, Sweet and Sour Mandarinfish and Crisp Eel.

Unit 9 Dessert

Part A
Focus on Language
Listening

Tapescript

Cakes

Cakes(1) are the highlight of many celebrations. What birthday(2) recipes would be complete without a cake with candles to blow out, or a wedding(3) without a beautiful cake to cut? Some of the most traditional cake(4) provide the best bases for decorating. None of the cakes involve complicated techniques, and several are as simple as putting the ingredients into a bowl, and mixing them together. Fruit cake(5) is one of our most popular special occasion cakes. Among its advantages is that it keeps really well and in fact improves with storage, so it can be baked well ahead of time and decorated(6) in easy stages. It also provides a wonderfully firm base for all sorts of elegant or novelty decorations. There are other ideas, too, for those who prefer a less rich tasting cakes, such as the Madeira or a light fruit cake, as well as a quick-mix sponge(7) for those last-minute, spontaneous celebrations.

2. Lining Cake Tins

Lining Cake Tins

Fill in the blanks with the word that you will hear on the tape.

Tapescript

Greaseproof paper is normally used for lining cake tins(1). The paper lining prevents the cakes from sticking(2) to the tins and makes them easier to turn out(3). Different cake recipes require slightly different techniques of linings, depending on the shape(4) of the tin, the type of cake mixture, and how long the cake needs to cook. Quick-mix(5) sponge cakes require only one layer(6) of paper to line the base, for example, whereas rich (7) fruit cakes that often bake for several hours if they are large in size need to be lined with a double layer of paper on the base(8) and sides. This extra protection also helps cakes to cook evenly.

Part B
Focus on Language
Listening

Tapescript

1. Sachertorte, one of the world's finest—and most famous—cakes, is a dark and delectable chocolate cake. It often serves in tiny slices for afternoon tea.

2. This fruit cake is made without saturated fat, yet retains the rich, familiar flavour of traditional fruit cakes.

3. A rich, creamy, American-style cheesecake, baked on a sweet biscuit base. It is topped with a selection of exotic fresh fruit; varies the decoration to suit the season.

4. Panforte is a specialty of Siena in Italy, where it is traditionally baked at Christmas. It is a combination of chopped candied peel and nuts, which are mixed with sugar syrup before baking.

5. Angel food cake is a true American classic. Although similar to a whisked sponge cake, it differs in that it contains no egg yolks. This results in a delicate snowy white texture.

Language Tips
2. Decorating with chocolate
Practice 2
Fill in the blanks with the word that you will hear on the tape.

Tapescript

Chocolate(1) decorations can look particularly interesting if different kinds of chocolate—dark, milk and white—are used in combination. White chocolate can be colored, but make sure you use powdered(2) food coloring for this as liquid(3) colorings will thicken it. Store chocolate decorations in the refrigerator in a plastic container(4) between layers of greaseproof paper until ready to use(5). Also, handle the decorations as little as possible with your fingers, as they will leave dull marks on the shiny surface of the chocolate.

Unit 10 Food Safety

Part A
Focus on Language
Listening

Listen to the tape and fill in the blanks with the words that you will hear on the tape.

Tapescript

Personal Hygiene Standards

All production staff members should wear uniforms(1) and preferably change into them when they report to work. They should wear hair restraints such as caps(2), chef's hats(3), or 4 hair nets(4). Smoking and eating should be prohibited in food preparation areas. The tasting of food(5) products is periodically necessary, but this must be done in a sanitary way. Utensils used for tasting should never be re-introduced to food products, and no one should use fingers to sample food. Hand-washing(6) is critical before, during, and after food preparation activities. Single-use gloves(7) should be worn when appropriate. Finally, unauthorized person(8)shouldn't be allowed in the food preparation area.

Do Extension Activities
Activity 1

Listen to the passage. Fill in the blanks with the word that you will hear on the tape.

Tapescript

Pests such as insects(1) and rodents(2) in kitchen are often just a nuisance; however, some can damage food (3) or possessions in your kitchen. Simple preventive(4) measures can stop most problems before they begin. Even when pests do get into kitchen, there is rarely a need to use pesticides(5). Simply removing their food supply(6) and breeding sites(7) is often the most effective control.

Steps such as managing garbage(8) so that it attracts fewer insects and animals, cleaning up(9) spilled food, and eliminating damp(10) conditions around the house are simple deterrents. It is good way to get rid of insects and rodents with a minimal amount of risk to health and the environment.

Part B
Start You Off
Activity 1

Listen to the passage carefully. Fill in the blanks with what you will hear.

Tapescript

Almost all food products are composed largely of organic material. Once the food is harvested or slaughtered, the organic material in it begins to break down (1) chemically. Spoilage organisms break down the complex organic substances in foods into their simple and inorganic components. This process is responsible for the changes in the odor(2), color(3), texture(4), appearance(5), and taste(6) of food products which indicate spoilage. Spoiled food is unfit for human consumption.

The spoilage of food products in a food establishment is often linked to one or more of the following causes:
- Improper storage temperatures(7)
- Incorrect or excessive storage times(8)
- Failure to segregate foods in storage
- Excessive delays(9) between the receiving and storing of food products
- Inadequate or unacceptable sanitation standards(10) resulting in exposure of food products to contaminants

As this list suggests, most food spoilage occurs when foods are at the storing control points. Storage area standards must be designed to prevent or minimize food spoilage and exposure of food products to pathogenic organisms.

Reference

1. Joanna Lorenz. The Practical Encyclopedia of Cakes & Cake Decorating Anness Publishing Limited 1999.
2. Ronald F. Cichy. Food Safety——Managing the HACCP Process By the Educational Institute of the American Hotel & Lodging Association.
3. Andrew E.Bennett (美). 饭店英语. 北京:外语教学与研究出版社. 2006.10.
4. Jack C.Richards, David Bycina, Sue Briouxaldcorn. 新英语交谈 北京:外语教学与研究出版社. 牛津大学出版社. 2004.9.
5. 蔡洁仪. 中西酱汁佳肴. 福建:福建科学技术出版社. 2004.2.
6. 郭亚东. 西餐工艺. 北京:中国轻工业出版社. 2000.2.
7. 《学做中国菜》编委会. 学做中国菜(水产类). 北京:外文出版社,1999.
8. 《学做中国菜》编委会. 学做中国菜(肉菜类). 北京:外文出版社,2000.
9. 黄福基. 意法美食. 福建:福建科学技术出版社. 2004.2.
10. 教育部《旅游英语》教材编写组,高等教育出版社. 2005.2.
11. 李秀斌. 现代餐饮英语实务教程. 北京:世界图书出版公司. 2007.9.
12. 李柏红,张小玲. 烹饪专业英语[M]. 北京:中国商业出版社,2006.
13. 李佳. 饭店英语. 北京:化学工业出版社. 2007.1.
14. 罗伯特·马杰尔. 餐饮英语[M]. 北京:旅游教育出版社,1999.
15. 罗伯特·马杰尔(陈亚丽等改编). 厨房英语[M]. 北京:旅游教育出版社,2006.
16. 赖声强. 名厨看家菜-西菜集萃. 上海:上海科技教育出版社. 2004.4.
17. 孙冰. 餐饮管理英语入门. 北京:清华大学出版社. 北京交通大学出版社. 2007.11.
18. 唐莉. 饭店情景英语. 北京:中国人民大学出版社. 2007.11.
19. 魏国富. 实用旅游英语教程.复旦大学出版社. 2005.3.
20. 邢怡. 餐饮英语. 北京:高等教育出版社. 2006.5.
21. 肖璇. 现代酒店英语实务教程. 北京:世界图书出版公司. 2007.9.
22. 冼宝勋. 串烧. 北京:海天出版社. 2007.8.
23. 闫文胜. 西餐烹调技术. 北京:高等教育出版社. 2006.8.
24. 张慧,孙玉瑞. 俄式西餐. 北京:中国建材工业出版社. 2005.4.

www.google.com wikipedia. the free encyclopedia